Advance Praise for *

"[Marc Pittman] is a new, powerful Southern voice whose compelling style of telling his great story about human relationships is unlike any you've ever read before. With each sentence, each paragraph, the reader discovers a world quite different from the frenetic, pell-mell lives of millions of today's families.

"Here's a father who early on determines that his two sons will not be reared the way his father treated him, treatment that would have broken the spirit and the will to achieve of most men. He painfully discovers a way back to living a worthwhile life as he witnesses the birth of first one son, then the other.

"Then tragedy strikes him and his family, and brings about disastrous human reactions. We see the author wrestling the bears in his life and struggling in the quagmire of 'Why me, God?' I found tears filling my eyes over how the Almighty came to intervene and led him and family members to a greater understanding than ever before. One of these days, I'll be making a journey to the memorial he erected along the highway where the crushing death of one of his sons occurred. . . .

"As a writer with published novels to my own credit, I can only bring roses to the altar of the new understanding I gained in reading this great work. It's a five-star read and should be in each reader's library for the 'must reread again section.' . . . The story gradually clutches at the soul to the point where it cannot be laid aside. It must be read to the last word."

—Lloyd Lenard
author, *Miracle on the 13th Hole*

Raising Cole

Developing Life's Greatest Relationship,
Embracing Life's Greatest Tragedy

A Father's Story

Marc Pittman
with Mark Wangrin

Health Communications, Inc.
Deerfield Beach, Florida

www.hcibooks.com

Library of Congress Cataloging-in-Publication Data

Pittman, Marc
    Raising Cole : developing life's greatest relationship, embracing life's
greatest tragedy / a father's story / Marc Pittman with Mark Wangrin.
      p. cm.
    ISBN-13: 978-0-7573-0202-2 (tp)
    ISBN-10: 0-7573-0202-5 (tp)
    1. Fathers and sons.   2. Parenting.   3. Grief.   4. Pittman, Brandon
Cole, 1980–2001.   I. Wangrin, Mark.   II. Title.

HQ756.P546 2004
306.874'2—dc22

                                          2004042489

Publisher: Health Communications, Inc.
             3201 S.W. 15th Street
             Deerfield Beach, FL 33442-8190

R-04-07

Cover design by Larissa Hise Henoch
Cover photo ©The University of Texas
Inside book design by Lawna Patterson Oldfield

This book is dedicated

To the memory of my son, Cole Pittman

To Judy Pittman, world's greatest mother

To Payton Cole Pittman, truly a gift from God

To Chase Pittman, who has been my lifeline

Marc Pittman

To Barbara, Makala and Ben, who remind me every

moment how fortunate I am

Mark Wangrin

CONTENTS

NOTHING IN LIFE IS AS difficult as burying a child. Marc Pittman has written a powerful and moving love story about his son Cole, who tragically died in an automobile accident at the tender age of twenty-one. Cole was an outstanding football player at the University of Texas. It was my privilege to have Cole and his family come into my life, never to leave.

This book traces Marc's tough upbringing and his transition into a compassionate, loving father through the gifts of his two sons. Although born of Cole's death, this book is not about death, but life—and the gift of life presented to each of us every day. This book touched me just as Cole Pittman touched all those who came into contact with him.

Darrell Royal
Former Football Coach, University of Texas

INTRODUCTION

THE HARDEST DAY OF MY life was the day I had to tell Marc Pittman we had lost his son, Cole.

It's not supposed to happen that way. As parents, we believe that our children will outlive us, and that is the way it should be. As coaches, we have always tried to run our football program on the premise that you can turn a crisis into a positive, and this was the biggest crisis of all.

But in that moment, we gained strength from those who were touched the most—Marc and Judy Pittman. We had lost a player and a friend; they had lost a son. I didn't understand it, and I still don't. I guess we are not supposed to understand everything in this life.

If, then, we are to take something tragic and turn it into something that serves a greater good, how can we do that? The answer the Pittmans gave us is that you do it with faith, friends and family.

As I sat at Cole's funeral, I remember the minister saying, "How many Saturdays do you have left?"

I started counting. *Let's see,* I thought. *I'm about fifty years old, and.* . . .

And then he stopped me.

"No, you don't know," he said. "Last Saturday may have been the last of your life."

Since Cole's death, I have reached out more to my kids and to other people. I have said "I love you" and have tried to listen and hug more. Cole died in a truck wreck on his way back to Austin. Since that day, we ask our players to check in with our coaches when they leave and when they arrive. Too many times in our business, our priority becomes winning. Cole's death reminds us that there are more important things than a football game. We have been privileged to have had both Cole and his younger brother, Chase, in our football program.

This book is the story of a father's love for his sons, his unique way of parenting and how it worked for him. The Pittmans gave a special definition to faith and love. Through the tough times and the good times, the way they went about showing that love has taught us and helped us all.

Mack Brown
Head Football Coach, University of Texas

PART ONE

*M*y son could always tell his daddy anything. No matter what the subject, no matter what the tone or the gravity, Cole Pittman could tell me. He could share his dreams without conceit and unburden his failings without fear.

Cole and I were tighter than most boys and their daddies; we were bonded, really, more than twins in the womb. "Me and my dad—I figure there is no other father and son in the United States closer than me and my dad," Cole once told a television reporter before catching himself. "You know, nobody in the world."

Growing up a son in my house in northwestern Louisiana meant participating in a common practice called Dead Man's Talk. Sprung out of the necessity of men-will-be-men frankness at a deer-hunting lease in nearby Minden, Louisiana, years ago, it was the ultimate in unvarnished no-tell confession. My friends and I would hunt all day and then gather in the small, simple huts at night to lay bare our souls and consciences, with no bag limit on the truth. We told of practical jokes we had played or how one of us had won a chili cook-off using dog food. We talked about *whatever we wanted, or needed, to say. There was only one catch: What we saw, what we heard—the names, dates, places and times—stayed there.*

When my oldest son was seven and my youngest boy, Chase, was three, I figured I could use this concept for child-rearing because it fit my one unwavering desire of parenthood: to be the kind of daddy I always wanted to have.

Under the rules, Cole and Chase could tell me anything and everything. I could have all the reaction of a dead man. What they told me could spark no spasms of anger, no lectures of right and wrong. There could be no reprisals. I could only listen and learn.

We shared most everything. Some of it made a father's heart swell with pride; some made it drop through his stomach. I heard some things I didn't want to hear, and every bit of what I needed to hear. Just as importantly, I told them things I'd never told anybody, the kind of things my father would never have shared with me.

I had loved my daddy, but he would never tell me what my boys were telling me, never even think it. Our relationship was fabricated out of my simple desire to get a small nod, or that vague look of satisfaction that I saw in my father's eyes even if nobody else did. Edward Pittman was a barrel-chested, five-foot-ten, 220-pound powerhouse who worked seven days a week as a farmer and millwright, didn't drink, smoked a pipe and remains to this day the only man ever to knock me unconscious, which he did twice. We were as poor as the dusty early nineteenth-century military supply road that ran by our farm. We raised what we ate, and my fifteen brothers and sisters and I slept three to a bed in a small white frame house with a tin roof.

When my dad needed something of me, his youngest son, I didn't hesitate. At my daddy's bidding I dug wells by hand in the hard red clay, worked my end of a crosscut saw all day with no relief and tore down wasps' nests with my bare hands. I got stung so many times that I learned to hold a wasp in my hands and laugh as it stabbed me.

Sometimes I got that nod.

I wanted my boys to get much more.

And so my sons and I had Dead Man's Talk about the grave and the trivial. We whispered as we cradled rifles high in a deer stand, or joked as we tooled around in the pickup truck or ate shrimp and spaghetti at Cole's favorite Italian restaurant. We shared our triumphs and embarrassments while lifting weights in a steamy gym or in the cool night air of the deck behind our Shreveport town home. As Cole grew from a peewee soccer star to a college football lineman at the University of Texas, we talked more often and covered more territory. I wanted nothing left unsaid. Nothing.

Once one of Cole's high school coaches, rankled that I may have had a too-perfect view of my son, pointedly suggested there were things I didn't know about his involvement in another boy's misdeeds.

"Oh, you talking about how he had dared the boy to shoplift?" I said.

The coach's eyes widened.

"You don't understand," I told him. "Cole tells me everything."

There now came a time for Cole to help me understand something I couldn't begin to grasp, to help me find the words to explain what I couldn't possibly fathom. On this night I laid down next to my son, pen and pad at the ready. It was my turn to unburden. In a few hours a man who only a few years earlier had gotten the sweats just at the thought of being called upon to pray in a small Bible study would be addressing several thousand people hanging on his every word. I never needed my son's help more.

Though I had brought along a pillow and blanket, I had no intention of sleeping. We talked through the night, through the cloud-shrouded dawn, through the rainy early morning. At 10 A.M. I finally left, to wash up, to take a deep breath, and to put on a white shirt, dark jacket and khaki slacks.

An hour later I returned, to find Cole just where I had left him. And after the music stopped, when the minister nodded at me that it was my turn to speak, I stepped up to the blue-silver casket, leaned over, kissed my boy and whispered, "Son, what should I say?"

ONE

Embracing the Pain

IT'S BEEN MORE THAN THREE years since I buried my oldest son in the red Louisiana dirt near Minden. Try as I might, I still can't recall much of what I said to the family, friends and mourners at First Assemblies of God sanctuary that gloomy Wednesday in February 2001.

What I can tell you is that Cole spoke to me that day. Cole spoke *through* me that day. He still does. In a way, he's speaking to you through this book. Cole and I still talk all the time, no matter where I'm at or what I'm doing. Sometimes I'm crouched in the mud at Fellowship Cemetery, my cheek leaning on his headstone. Sometimes I'm pacing the shoulder on Highway 79 just north of Franklin, Texas, tracing the last few hundred feet where the tires of his pickup truck flattened the grass as they drifted off the road. Sometimes I'm polishing the large oak cross I erected at the crash site, the one with the plaque that reads, "In life he touched the world, in death he rocked it." Sometimes I'm just laying awake in the dark.

I'm fifty years old. I am a millwright and a construction worker. My entire life I have been a man who worked with his hands fixing things. If a house needed a new roof I shingled it. If a room needed to be enlarged I knocked out a wall and added on. If a support beam was sagging I shored it up. Again and again I fixed what was broken and changed what I couldn't fix, from cracked panes of glass to the way I approached and lived my life. That's what I was good at. That's what I did.

On the morning of February 26, 2001, God gave me something I couldn't fix or change. My son, a junior defensive tackle at the University of Texas, fell asleep behind the wheel of his 1997 red Chevrolet pickup truck while returning for the first day of spring football practice. Sometime around 7:30 A.M., his truck veered off Highway 79, hit a guardrail, flipped and landed upside-down in a brush-covered creek bed. I pray he died instantly.

People are always asking me how I'm doing, how I'm handling the grief of losing my boy. The truth is that we do not pay much attention to our soul. Neither do we pay much attention to our fingers, our hands or our eyes until they are bruised or

battered. Then that part of our physical being becomes important. When you bury your son, your soul is bruised. God is the
only source of comfort to ease that pain, which is why I embrace
the pain, because God shows up and helps me through it.

I've buried my father, my mother, cousins and a niece. I
watched my sister die from a two-year struggle with breast cancer. I found my nephew in a field, dead of a shotgun wound to
the head. Add up all that pain, multiply it by a billion, and it
wouldn't scratch the surface of losing Cole Pittman.

The people who ask mean well, I know. It's not always what
you say to comfort someone; it's just the fact you're saying
something. They try to understand, but they can't, just as I can't
understand what it's like for any other father who has lost his
son. Every relationship is different, every loss unique. I can only
tell you how I tried to handle it.

How we handle pain determines whom we become. For me
there was only one approach: Meet the pain head on. Don't duck
it. Embrace it. Drown in it. Let it smother you until you can
smother it. Coping with death, to me, is all about remembering
love. I don't worry about the pain. I'll worry if I ever stop feeling the pain.

I was blessed to have a son like Cole, and I'm doubly blessed
that even in death Cole can continue to touch people. After he
died I received hundreds of letters, phone calls and e-mails,
most of them from people I didn't know. Somehow, some way,

they had heard of our story. President George W. Bush sent a note. The chancellor of the University of Texas's fiercest rival, Texas A&M, sent his condolences. Notre Dame sent a card signed by the entire football team.

Many of the responses came from people from all walks of life who had heard our story from friends or read newspaper articles about Cole. They weren't football fans, had no ties to the University of Texas and had only one common bond. They, too, wanted to build better relationships with their loved ones. A woman doctor in Houston, a single parent, wrote that she pasted the Prayer of Jabez on her refrigerator after reading a newspaper story that talked of its importance in our relationship. A woman who was in the San Diego airport the morning after Cole's last game in the Holiday Bowl had seen a young man—Cole—playing with some little kids while his teammates slept. A preacher in Kansas City sent me a basket of breads and jellies along with a note that said for months after I visited his church he still received requests for copies of the tape of my remarks there.

People always tell me one other thing, after they ask how I'm doing. They tell me what a special bond I had with Cole, how it's touched them and made them work harder to have the same relationship with their children. They tell me I was lucky. Maybe I was, but I worked at it too.

Those people want me to tell them how we grew so close. They want to know how I could convince my boys to tell me everything; how our love would be so without compromise that they would think nothing of kissing me on the mouth in front of eighty-three thousand people or holding hands in our truck as we drove around town.

We did Dead Man's Talk because I didn't want the emptiness and silence I had with my father. When my boys buried me I didn't want them to feel that anything was left unsaid. I wanted a relationship with honesty and trust. With work, we were able to build that. Anybody, if willing to work at it, can do it too, and not just with sons but with daughters and brothers and sisters and parents and anybody else they want to pull closer.

We fought what we called Love Wars, where a spoken "I love you" was answered with a salvo of "I love you more" and escalated from there. We were always trying to outdo each other in showing our love, not only by words but also by actions and sacrifices. It's an approach that can work in any human relationship, bringing peace and satisfaction I can't even begin to describe. I never wanted to win the war, but I sure couldn't stand to lose it.

We listened. Many a time my sons recalled a lesson I had taught them long before, when I didn't think they were paying attention. I learned how important it was to mean what you say and say what you mean, and how relationships are built like houses. No building, no matter how well constructed, will stand without a solid, well-laid foundation. Honesty was our concrete;

openness and trust our rebar. Relationships don't just happen. They're built.

The foundation of my relationship with my father was made of fear and respect. Neither love nor affection ever figured in the mixture. That's like trying to mix a good load of concrete without sand or gravel. My father never told me that he loved me, never showed me any affection except the occasional pat on the head. God, how I wished I would have heard him say it just once.

Often I hear people talk about how they don't grow close to their kids because they never had a father to learn from. You don't need a father to teach you. All you need is a heart, a resolve and one simple guideline: Be the father you always wanted to have.

I am blessed in that I have another son, Chase, and we have become as close or closer than Cole and I were. Ten months after Cole's death, Chase followed his brother to the University of Texas. He lockers one cubicle away from where his brother did, plays the same position Cole did as a freshman and drives the same road that took Cole to his death every time he makes a trip home. Chase hugs the pain in the same eyes-wide, chin-up, chugging-life-at-110-miles-per-hour embrace that I do.

Forgetting the pain would mean forgetting my son. Cole Pittman lives as long as he's not forgotten. I want as many people as possible to remember him for as long they live. Call me selfish. I want him to live forever.

T W O

Learning to Lose

I WAS BORN ON JULY 30, 1952, to Edward Pittman and his wife Clotile. There wasn't any fanfare, with ten children preceding me and five more to follow, but when the thirteenth child—one of my twelve sisters—was born a few years later, friends and neighbors came calling. Having a thirteenth child was a big event in those parts. Figuring we'd sent enough money their way on the previous dozen, neither the doctor nor the hospital would charge a fee. That's a pretty big deal when you're too poor to be having kids anyway.

When I was four we moved to an old white frame house, hard by an old road that General Andrew Jackson had blazed as a supply route during the War of 1812. I heard that the road led all the way to Arkansas, but for me it didn't much matter, seeing as how we were poor and going to stay poor, right there in Dubberly, Louisiana.

The house was an old shotgun shack, raised high enough off the ground for a small child to run under it. At one time the house had a dog run, which is a breezeway that separates the living quarters from the sleeping quarters, one that's open at both ends so a dog could run through it. It was the nicest home I'd ever seen. It actually had paint on the exterior, canvas wallpaper with a pretty floral print and a bathtub. It had beautiful redbud bushes around the sides and hedges around the front porch. There was a huge oak tree out back.

We raised our own vegetables and had a few cows we milked, but that was the extent of our luxuries. I remember my dad once saying after blessing the food, "We are blessed here. We have a thousand things to eat, but they are all peas." When we ran out of peas we ate dried beans. My dad was old-school. He didn't allow a loaf of bread or any bought bread inside the house, so my mom cooked seventy-three biscuits every morning for breakfast.

I learned to elbow at the dinner table to get my share of biscuits. I also learned to work without complaint and to hide my pain. I learned too that I didn't fit in, not at school, and not with my brothers and sisters. They must have sensed my problems with self-esteem because most of them jumped on and never let up. One of my brothers, about three years older than me, would join his friends in calling me "queer" and "weirdo" and would help them beat me up, giving me what we called "the corner treatment." They'd drag me into a corner, where the bigger kids, mostly juniors and seniors, would turn their class rings around and use them as brass knuckles while the younger kids formed a wall to shield what was happening from the teachers. I'm not so sure the teachers purposely didn't look away anyway.

I was being taught not to like myself, too. Unlike my school-work, at that I was a quick study. In eighth grade I was only five-foot-six, and I had a teacher who kept telling me I'd never be as tall as my older brother, who was six-five. She kept telling me I'd never be this, never be that, just bombarding me with nega-tives. To this day I wonder how many teachers out there don't realize the damage they can do to kids by constantly feeding them negatives.

My social life, if you could call it that, was grim. I didn't have a date in high school, unless you count some ride-the-bus-courting—a little smooching on the school bus after I'd become a success as a basketball player my senior year. Even if I'd had a date, I had no way to get there. Mother never let me borrow the car, not even to take it a mile or two down the road. We're not talking about a Rolls Royce, either, just a '59 Chevy Biscayne in which you could see the highway by looking not only through the windshield and the back window, but also through the floor-board, at least when it wasn't choked with exhaust smoke.

Now, when I look back, I'm amazed at how I reacted. The worse my family treated me, the higher I put them above me. I was on a mission to be accepted by my family, to get some kind of approval, but the harder I tried, the deeper the wedge between us grew.

One day my older brother Bill threw a book across the table and it slid into a window, breaking it. My dad came in, saw the window and asked Bill who broke it. Bill just looked at him. Daddy turned to me and asked the same question. Now I didn't want to be a tattletale, but then again I was afraid to lie to my daddy. "Bill did," I finally said.

Bill got a whipping in front of everybody. It was a good one, too. Daddy could be ruthless when he whipped us, and he didn't spare anything on Bill. It didn't take long before everyone was staring at me with loathing for being a tattletale. I couldn't take it. I grabbed my daddy's arm and yelled, "I did it! I did it!"

Daddy raised his arm. I got the whipping—and a look from my brothers and sisters that meant I deserved it. I never told any of them who broke the window. Bill, as was his way, never did either.

When I was fifteen I took a job at Public Liquidators in Shreveport, hitchhiking the forty-five miles there and back. When I couldn't land a ride, I'd sleep in the back alley in the furniture truck or, when I felt a little more resourceful, I'd undo the fire doors and sneak into the furniture store, where I'd crash on a real bed. At the end of the summer I took most of the money I saved and bought a motorcycle from a guy who had wrecked it when he slid into a post trying to avoid a train.

I eventually wrecked it myself, and this time there was no way to put it back together. I survived, but that was no great surprise to my mother. She considered me unkillable.

My mom was a five-foot, seven-inch French Cajun woman, and she could match my dad for work ethic and toughness. When she milked the cows, the force was so strong that the foam spilled over the top before the bucket was even half full. I had heard that when she went into labor with me, she was shelling peas in the kitchen. She put them on the stove, left the kitchen to give birth to me, then came back and took them off the stove.

For some reason, as I was growing up, I never was one of my mother's favorite people. She made it clear to me that she never thought I'd amount to anything. In fact, for a long time I think she saw me as just another mouth to feed. It was that way with her and her mom, too. My grandmother always used to badmouth my mother to her sisters, but it was my mother who took care of her as she was dying of cancer. Grandma's eye had swollen to where it had burst and the house smelled of death, but my mother kept trying.

On her deathbed Grandma called for her. "This is Clotile," one of my aunts said to ease her fears, but Grandma said, "No.

Clotile, the one who loved me, who took care of me. I want Clotile." All the pain she had ever given my mother was vindicated right then.

Like me, my mother was devoted to my daddy, holding on to his memory long after his death. The night before she died I told her, "It's okay to go be with Daddy. We'll be okay."

Mom and I made our peace late in life, and when she died I was chosen as the family spokesperson. My family was adamant that I keep the eulogy short, so I did, trying to please them. Later on, I was ashamed. My mother of forty-four years, who raised sixteen children and many times went silently hungry while I ate the last biscuit, surely deserved much more than three minutes. I don't think anybody else could have done what she did as well as she did it. We all should have spoken, for as long as we felt was right.

THREE

Man Was Born to Die

M Y DADDY WAS A GRUFF, tough, no-nonsense island of a man, part Irish and part Cherokee. He had the bluest eyes that I'd ever seen, ones that could pierce right through you, but with a soft sensitivity that made people feel he cared. It made me feel he cared, anyway. For my first twenty-nine years he was the most important person in my life.

You may find that statement odd, because growing up I never spent much free time with my father. There were a few Sundays after church we spent splashing around at Shaw's Pond, the local swimming hole, or spent a Sunday afternoon driving around looking for deer tracks. There just wasn't time to do much more. My daddy and rust worked the same hours.

We never did have much, but I admired the way my daddy carried himself with pride, shoulders back and chest out. I admired his toughness. I was in awe of the way he could, and did, stare down sheepdogs, cur dogs, attack dogs, you name it. He'd look them in the eye, show no fear. They'd hunker down and crawl backwards. Later, after he'd died, when I was searching for a reason to live, I would try to develop that look to intimidate other men.

People said the Pittman girls got all the brains and the beauty in the family. I used to say that if cancer didn't kill my dad, pride in those girls would have made him burst. Maybe it would have, but I think Daddy was equally proud of his boys.

He called me "Man-Boy" because I worked harder than my years would suggest. I was the youngest boy, and I would do anything to please him, from catching a wasp and saying it didn't hurt when it stung me, to carrying fence posts as big around and twice as long as me, to plowing all day long even while full-grown men took breaks in the beating sun. Around Christmastime our class at school would draw names and exchange presents, with a fifty-cent limit. I'd know that the cost of a gift, no matter how nominal, was a burden on the family. I'd always ask for .22-caliber cartridges or rifle ammunition for hunting, so I could rewrap it and give it to my dad. Anything to get his approval.

When I played basketball at Dubberly High School, my dad would come watch me play. I never heard him cheer, but that wasn't important. He was there. After the games he'd try to take me out for a Coke. I knew Cokes cost a dime. I knew how little money we had. I said no.

To me, my daddy was larger than life. Nobody could say a word against him. If someone at school said they could whip my daddy, the fight was on. Nobody could whip my daddy.

My father's background is somewhat of a mystery because he never talked about it. I knew he was an orphan, raised by his grandparents. I suspect, piecing together things I'd heard here and there, that he killed a man. Apparently two brothers of a girl he was dating didn't take kindly to her taste in male companionship and jumped him. The story has it that one ended up dying. According to the story, my daddy ran.

While I didn't know much of his background, I knew the man he'd become. "Pain is what we are," he'd tell me. "Pain is who we become." Funny, though, he never showed much pain. Even later, when the cancer had him all swollen up, when the skin of his ankles lapped over the top of his shoes, he still worked. He was all about toughness and all about reliability, asking for no charity and accepting none.

I've grown to be six-foot, six-inches and 268 pounds, and I still have the same thirty-six-inch waist I had when I was twenty-two. I've had more than my share of fights, some fair, others not, but to this day my daddy remains the only man to have ever knocked me out. He did it with one punch. Twice. Neither time was it my fault.

The first time I was sixteen. He had just come in from work and was reading the newspaper when I turned around. My shoulder hit him on the bridge of his nose, which was already sore from wearing glasses. When I came to he was standing over me, just looking down. He never said he was sorry. It wasn't his way. But he didn't have to. There was so much pain in his face, and it wasn't from my shot to his nose. The pain was from striking me, knowing how much I loved him. He didn't know how to say he was sorry.

It was the same a year or two later, when he was dying of cancer and I slapped him on his backside as a hello. He didn't say he was sorry then either, just as he never told me he loved me. He didn't know how to say that either. That day I learned a life lesson. You have to be able to express your feelings. If you keep it all bottled up inside, it'll destroy you.

Inability to express himself didn't destroy him. Liver cancer got him first.

It was 1971, and I was eighteen. I had always struggled with my self-image, but now, fresh out of high school, things were looking up. I had a job working as a carpenter for my brother, making the princely sum of $1.75 an hour. I bought my first truck, a green 1951 Chevrolet pickup, and had my first date. Within six to eight months I'd traded up to a '66 Super Sport. My dating had picked up, too.

Late that summer my daddy went into the hospital for gallstone surgery. They opened him, took one look and closed him right back up. They gave him six to eight weeks to live. I think he lived six.

At the time my daddy was working at the Louisiana Army Ammunition Plant, and he'd tell me about the tools he used, the things he did. We never talked about the cancer. I couldn't bear to sit and visit with him as he became weaker and weaker. Seeing such a strong man waste away hurt me, so I bought him one of those little gripper things, two plastic handles connected by a coil of steel, that are used to improve hand strength. I watched as he struggled to squeeze it. Without thinking, I grabbed it from him and started popping it like it was nothing. I'll never forget the look in his eye. What I thought would impress him had destroyed him. For the first time, I saw a look of defeat in his eyes. I don't think I've ever regretted anything more.

A few weeks later he woke my mother in the middle of the night and told her she needed to take him to the hospital. Daddy didn't want to die in the house with the kids there.

The next day, I went to see my daddy for what I knew was the last time. He knew it too. He was talking incoherently, just bab-bling, but he made me promise I wouldn't sell one of the horses that I had started riding, a quarterhorse named Shane. Then I bent over and kissed him good-bye and told him, for the first time in my life, that I loved him.

With my mind clouded in fear and my eyes in tears, I drove off and turned north on a southbound street. When I reached the top of the hill, it nearly ended for me right there in a head-on collision. Several cars waited while I backed the car down the road, probably a quarter of a mile.

Somehow I made it back to Dubberly. It was just after noon. I was sitting in the den with Mrs. Jones, my brother-in-law's mother, making strained small talk when I heard the most beautiful sound. It came from a bird in the big chinaberry tree outside the house, one I'd never heard before. Mrs. Jones looked at me.

"Isn't that beautiful?" she said.

"My daddy just died," I said.

I'd hardly gotten the words out of my mouth when the hospital called.

The next few days were a blur. I watched numbly as some of my brothers and sisters walked around, some truly broken-hearted, some filled with self-importance as they talked about how they would help my mother, something they needn't worry about. She was tough as nails. As usual, I wasn't included in these discussions, but it didn't matter. I was lost in my own thoughts, thinking about the only wisdom he really ever saw fit to dispense.

"Man was born to die," he always told me.

He was my best friend and my hero. I believed him.

FOUR

Lost Along the Way

M Y MOTHER ALWAYS SAID I was unkillable.

"I always worry about something happening to my chirrin', but I don't worry 'bout you," she said in her French Cajun accent. "If you was goin' to die, it'd happened a long time ago."

She might have had something there. In my life I've survived being hit by a van and having a 250-pound scaffolding fall five stories down an elevator shaft on top of me. I've wrestled bears and swam to within stare-down distance of a twelve-foot alligator. I probably should have been killed many times over now.

It sure wasn't for lack of trying.

When my father died of liver cancer, I lost my only reason for living. He was my hero, my role model. He gave me my only feeling of self-worth. Without anything else even resembling a healthy relationship in my life, there was no love worth treasuring.

After he passed away I would go to his grave just to be close to him. I felt he was still someone who could intercede for me here on earth. I felt I could tap his strength, his wisdom. He would point me in the right direction. He would watch over me.

Around me, life went on. People expressed their sorrow, but they moved on. They couldn't understand how I felt, what I had lost. Truth be told, I couldn't understand it either.

I began to numb myself with alcohol. Many a night I'd go out drinking, only to end up at Fellowship Cemetery, where I'd sob in the darkness. I'd ask God why. How could I fill the emptiness? Sometimes I'd just sit down on the grass. Sometimes I'd pass out, my head leaning against my mother's side of the family headstone, waking up at dawn when the shotguns went off to scare the deer from the nearby watermelon patches. Sometimes I'd ask for Daddy's help. "If you could just intercede for me up there," I'd say, "I could be up there with you. I just don't have the guts to do it myself."

As you can tell, I'd become pretty good at feeling sorry for myself. My temper was equipped with a hair trigger, and my solution to every affront was to fight. I don't know how many times I defended the honor of a woman I didn't know, just for a chance to mix it up. Sometimes a guy would up the ante and pull a handgun on me, waving it in my face and trying to get me to back down. I tried to stare him down the way my daddy used to stare down dogs. If that didn't work, I'd just laugh like a lunatic and slap the gun out of his hands.

I'd do crazy things. Randy Reagan, my running buddy, and I would drive up behind a lumber truck, the grill of my truck almost nudging its bumper. Randy would crawl over the hood and leap on the back of the truck. Once aboard, he'd get the chainsaw that was always strapped near the back, carry it over the logs to the cab, crawl over the cab and deposit the chainsaw on the front hood. Then he'd run back, jump back in the truck and tell me about the stunned look on the driver's face. We'd have a good laugh.

Early one morning, after a night of rolling dice, we took a '58 Chevy truck and took turns running up the railings on the side of a bridge trying to flip the truck for no better reason than to see if we could. Another time, totally sober but no less numb, I figured the solution to unclogging a three-foot pipe filled with wood pulp residue was to cut it open with a Skil saw. When I made the first cut, water spewed out and soon I was standing knee deep in water operating an electric saw. I burned out three saws cutting that pipe, but the cord never hit the water. I knew I could be electrocuted. I heard people call me an idiot. I just laughed.

I had made the biggest discovery of my life . . . to that point. I had found the ultimate high. It wasn't the alcohol, and I've never taken drugs. The high was to be absolutely fearless of death. Live, die—it didn't matter. The closer I came to dying, the bigger the high.

Why I didn't die I'll never know. Part of me certainly wanted to. Deep down, though, I felt that I had some deep, indescribable feeling that I wasn't supposed to die. Destiny had other plans for me. I would be a father.

This knowledge didn't give me any more direction. I was twenty-five and had a well-paying job helping to build a paper mill in Campti, Louisiana. But I was bored. I was tired of the bar scene, tired of drinking, tired of running the roads. Most of the money I earned I gave to my mother with the only condition that she pay my car note. What she did with the rest didn't matter to me.

And then I met Judy.

Judy Poisso was the most naive and innocent girl I'd ever dated. From the beginning, I knew Judy would make a wonderful mother. She's strong but compassionate, and she came to understand how deeply I wanted to become the daddy I never had. Instead of being jealous of the relationships I would build with our sons, she embraced them.

I've certainly made more than my share of mistakes in my life. Most of the wisdom we acquire comes from the mistakes we make instead of the things we do right. As I look over our marriage, one of the biggest mistakes we both made was that we were so focused on being good parents that we didn't devote enough time to our marriage. I could write a whole book about Judy, our relationship and her role in raising our boys. Maybe someday I will, but this book isn't about her. I will say this: If I could live my life over again, choose any woman to be the mother of my children, I'd pick Judy again, no question about it.

Of course, we didn't hit it off very well at first. Judy was a nursing student with whom my sister had tried to fix me up a year before. The first time we went out I think she was just trying to put me in my place. I had dated her suitemate, and her suitemate felt I'd misled her as to my intentions. Judy was going to teach me a lesson.

She soon realized I didn't mislead anybody. I was just tied down to nothing. If a girl wanted to go somewhere, we went there. If she wanted to do something, we did it. My self-esteem was still pretty low, and despite my rough-and-tumble reputation, I didn't like hurting people. That didn't include people who tried to pick a fight with me, or who mistreated others. Intimidation, I guess, was how I survived.

Judy was twenty-five, an age when women think about getting married. I figured that was okay with me. When she decided she wanted to get married, we just got married. It was as simple as that.

The night before our wedding, after the rehearsal dinner, her brothers and I hit the bars. *One last drunk wouldn't hurt anything,* I thought. Some of my sisters had been telling Judy they felt sorry for her, that I was a brute: rough, outspoken and insensitive. I can't say at the time I didn't agree. Part of me didn't want to make her life miserable by marrying her. A smaller part of me thought that maybe I could finally prove my family wrong that I was destined to fail at everything I did.

We drank. We drank some more. We got in a brawl. One brother-in-law had his throat slashed. Another had his head busted open by a whiskey bottle. A third had his teeth knocked out. I wound up with a broken hand, bruised face and two black eyes. They say we won the fight. Me? I was too drunk to know or care.

FIVE

My Son, My Son, My Son

N INETEEN MONTHS AFTER WE MARRIED, on January 26, 1980, I fulfilled what I thought I was brought in this world to do. Actually, Judy did the hard part, enduring eighteen hours of labor without any painkillers to bear our ten-pound, eight-ounce son, but at the time I felt the credit was all mine.

I held my boy in my hands in the labor and delivery room at Natchitoches Parish Hospital and said, "My son, my son, my son," a song of awe and reverence. I thought those were the most profound words anybody had ever uttered. I still feel that way, although I know now millions of people had uttered them before me, and a few million more since.

My brother Edward had already named his son Edward Pittman III so I was unable to honor my father that way, but I knew another man whose name was well worth carrying.

When I was nineteen I played in some area basketball leagues. Through those games I met a young man who was basketball coach at Glenbrook Christian Academy. Jerry Brandon, whom everyone called "The Blond Bomber," was a tall, lean former player only a year or two removed from Louisiana Tech. One time when we played his team, he was late getting to the gym. We were up by what seemed like forty points before he arrived. But when he walked in, the team responded to him, played harder and wound up beating us. He had an uncanny knack of relating to the kids, knowing how to push their buttons. They simply idolized him. I did too.

I was so insecure and so taken by his ability to be such a tremendous father figure that I decided then and there that when I had a boy I would name him after Jerry Brandon. When our first son was born I talked it over with Judy, and we decided to name him Brandon Cole Pittman.

A few years after Cole was born, I heard Jerry had been killed in a one-car accident near Minden. Jerry left behind a three-year-old son and a wife who was seven months pregnant. He would have been a fantastic father, I'm sure. He, not I, was the kind of man I wanted my son to be like.

I set my sights on providing for my family, just as my daddy had done. That meant a roof over their heads, food on the table and, when events required, a whipping for my boy. The price for that meant working long hours, though unlike my daddy I was making good money. I didn't need to work so much, at least not in a monetary sense.

For the next year-and-a-half I worked eighteen hours a day at my job as a millwright and precious little at being a father. Work was my excuse for not spending time with my son. I left the loving to his mother, who had plenty of love to spare. I'd smile at him and pat him on his little blond head. Love him? Yeah, I loved him like my daddy had loved me. Just like my daddy had loved me.

When I looked at Cole, as we called him, I didn't see a little boy wanting a father to show him love and affection, like I had secretly wanted my daddy to show me. Cole wanted that, of course, just as all little boys do, but what I saw was a pain I didn't want to revisit. The less time I could spend with him the better, because I knew the more I was around him the closer I'd get. I was scared, deathly scared, that I'd lose him. Sure as I'd get close to the boy, he'd die just like my daddy did.

Even with the money we were making, Judy and I hit hard times. We overreached and built a nice house, but interest rates soared from 10.5 to over 20 percent, and we were in a bind. We couldn't sell the house, but couldn't afford to keep it. We lost everything.

My financial bottom line wasn't the only one that showed a net loss. Self-esteem was still a problem, and I still reacted to those insecurities by not taking any guff from anyone. If I couldn't feel good about myself emotionally or spiritually through interactions with other people, I'd at least get the physical satisfaction of beating them up.

When Cole was a toddler, I was still helping build that paper mill in Campti, Louisiana. Like at any other work site, there was a rivalry between the construction crew and the mill crew. Each side had its designated tough guy. I was the construction crew's hooking bull. Whenever a challenge came up, I was expected to settle it. Some mill worker would say something, one of my construction buddies would take offense, and the next thing you knew we'd be hunched over a table, arm-wrestling for an eight-hundred-dollar, winner-take-all pot.

One day I was headed into work when I stopped for coffee at a little restaurant near the mill that was a favorite hangout of the workers, the Little Chief Café. Some of the mill crew and their tough guy, a black fellow who ran the supply room where the construction workers signed out magnetic drills, saws, whatever equipment we needed, were sitting around. I starting razzing him about something, I can't even remember what. It was something we had done hundreds of times before, and I thought this time was no different. But the man was hurting inside, racked by family problems. His marriage was falling apart, and when I verbally pushed him, he did more than push back.

"If you come outside," he said, his voice cracking, "I'll kill you."

He went outside and headed for his truck. I wasn't going to back down.

I followed him out.

The guy pulled a .38-caliber revolver out from under the driver's seat. Tears welled in his eyes, and his hands were shaking as he pointed it at my head.

I'd been in that situation before. First you get an adrenaline rush, the feeling that you just may be fixing to die. Then you feel like you're going to wet your pants, but that feeling quickly passes. You don't want to die like that, showing fear. You want to die like a man.

"You have three choices," I said sternly. "You can shoot me. You can drive off. Or I'll have to take it away from you."

Sobbing, he lowered the gun, tossed it back in his truck and drove off.

I stood there, feeling foolish and lucky and mortal. I realized I didn't want to die like a man just yet. I didn't want to die, period. I thought of my son, how he depended on me. I thought of what my father meant to me and what a father means to a boy.

A few days later, I was at home when I looked up to see my eighteen-month-old boy toddling around a corner. Cole was a dressed in a tiny taupe jogging suit with green stripes down the side, a huge guileless smile on his face, and all his innocence and needs and wants registered at once. *My son, my son, my son* sounded pretty hollow to me right then.

I have to be a daddy to this boy, I thought. In my heart I knew I already had the secret to being a good daddy. All the repressed feelings and hopes I had about what I wanted my daddy to say to me, how I wanted a hug or nod or kind word, just came bubbling up.

I would be the kind of daddy I always wanted to have.

———

It didn't take long to realize that the epiphany was the easy part.

For nearly all my life, I was secure in an underlying belief that fate would have me father two sons. For almost as long, I had steeled myself against the prospect of having any kind of close relationship with them. Changing my thought process, thinking of their needs and wants instead of mine, would take work. I was used to hard work, but this job would also take time and patience. It may have been the hardest thing I've ever done.

I wanted to be the kind of father I had wanted to have. I had wanted a father who would show me and tell me he loved me. I had wanted a father I could talk to. I had wanted a father who would discipline me when I needed it, build me up when I was low and reel me in if I went too far.

Now I just had to figure out how to make myself into that father.

I quit my job and convinced Judy that if we moved back to Minden everything would be okay. We were still struggling financially, trying to pay for a house we had started building and weren't even able to live in. Fortunately, Judy was able to land a job as director of nursing at a Winnfield nursing home, which included the use of a house. We struck a deal with the mortgage holder of the house we'd bought near Natchitoches that we'd pay them off when we were able to sell. They agreed, and we moved to Minden.

Cole became my shadow. I took him everywhere, except when I was on my new job as foreman of a construction crew. If I went hunting, he rode on my back. If I was working around the house, he was right there beside me.

Working.

When he was two years old, I taught him how to stand up in the driver's seat of our Jeep, strapped a seat belt around him and taught him to hold the wheel steady as we pulled a big float wagon. He'd drive it through the field as I loaded hay on the wagon, daring him to run over a bale.

At first it was the work that bonded us, just as it did my daddy and me. My daddy had never told me he loved me and certainly had never kissed me. My relationship with Cole was starting out the same way, and I assumed that was pretty much the way it was between fathers and sons. We had what at the time seemed to be the perfect basis for a relationship. I needed somebody to help me around the house. He was always right there underneath my feet. So I just used him. Worked him like a slave.

I could tell he enjoyed being around me, and I loved the time we spent together. When his friends and cousins were around, instead of playing with them he would rather stay with me, even if I was cutting firewood or plowing. No matter what I was doing, he'd rather stay with me than play with his friends. Watching him made me reflect on how I had felt about getting my daddy's approval. So I began to pat him on the head and hug his neck. More and more I began to kiss him and tell him how proud I was of him. Those were the things I had wanted my dad to do so badly. The more I patted his head, hugged his neck, kissed his lips, the more he wanted to do things for me and show me he loved me.

I was hooked.

SIX

Taketh and Giveth

W HEN MY DADDY DIED, I tasted pain like I'd never tasted before. That pain shaped my life, shaped my early attitudes on being a father. I swore I'd never get close to my boys, because just as soon as I did I'd lose them.

Then Cole was born, and I began learning how to be a real father to him. Three years later, just as Cole was breaking down all the barriers I had built, Judy was pregnant again.

I knew it would be a boy, and I told everybody that. Well, this rough-hewn female barber named Dot had a barbershop near where Judy worked at Evergreen Ministries, a facility for the mentally impaired. Dot wore boots, chewed tobacco, raised pheasants and peacocks, and cussed like a mule driver. When the unions in Minden wanted to raise the price of haircuts, she refused to go along and moved her business north of town.

One day I told her Judy was pregnant, and she asked if I'd like to know if it was a boy or girl. Smugly, I told her I knew it would be a boy. She told me to send Judy by and we'd find out for sure.

Judy came by Dot's, and she swung this pendulum, which she'd ordered out of some catalog, that was supposed to determine the sex of the fetus. Some special apparatus. It was just a ring on a chain. The guideline was something like if it swung in a circle it was a boy, but if it swung back and forth it was a girl.

Dot held it over Judy. It did the boy thing. Dot said it had never been wrong. "You're going to have a boy," she said.

A few weeks later we were at the doctor's for an ultrasound, a little bit more sophisticated than a ring on a chain. But totally inaccurate—at least that's what I thought when he told us he was "99 percent sure" it was a girl. He told us he normally didn't do predictions, but he just didn't see any of the male hardware.

Later he told Judy he'd never seen a man turn pale so quickly.

The next time I went for a haircut I told Dot the doctor said it was a girl. She thought maybe Cole was standing too close the first time she did the test so she had Judy come in for another try. When Judy arrived, Dot grabbed the pet peacock that sat on the Coke machine and told Cole to take him outside to catch some grasshoppers. Once again she swung the chain over Judy's belly. Clenching a pipe between her teeth, Dot looked straight at me.

"That little SOB may not be hung like a stud mule, but it's going to be a little boy," she grunted. "I've already told you the end of that story."

And so it was. Benjamin Chase Pittman was born, all twelve pounds and twenty-two inches of him, on March 15, 1983.

—◆—

I went about building my relationship with both my sons. I opened my heart to them. I vowed I'd never look back, never second-guess getting close to them. And I never did.

Not even after I almost lost both of them.

When Cole was four and Chase was just a baby, Judy and I decided we needed to build a home. We found some property and put up a mobile home to live in while I built the house right behind it.

First I had to clear the land. I brought a bulldozer home from the job one weekend and set about digging a deep pit to bury all the brush, tree stumps and other debris from clearing the lot. My plan was to move the debris into a pile and dig a pit next to it. Then I'd push up a pile of clay in front of the debris and roll it all into the pit.

As the pit got deeper and deeper, the red clay dirt pushed higher and higher in front of the blade. It was impossible to see much of anything in front of the bulldozer. I was almost done digging the pit when it was time for lunch. Normally I wouldn't have stopped. I like to finish what I start, and there were only a few more passes before the pit was deep enough.

I gave in and decided to stop and eat lunch. As I got off the bulldozer, I asked Judy where Cole was because I wanted to have lunch with my boy. Cole was supposed to stay inside, because I knew I couldn't see much behind the big mound of clay I was pushing up.

He wasn't in the house. Judy said she didn't know where he was.

Something caught in my heart. I raced around the huge mound of dirt to the pit. I could only see one finger sticking out of the dirt pile. The dirt was mostly clay and you peeled it off inches at a time. One more push with the bulldozer and that finger would have been buried.

Frantically I began trying by hand to dig him out of the packed clay. He had fallen straight back, arms extended and his face was under about a foot and a half of clay. I dug like a dog. I screamed for Judy. She collapsed in a heap at the trailer's steps.

I don't know how long it took me to get to him. I saw his nose and I quickly cleared the clay from around his face and opened his eyes. The pupils were fixed. His mouth was open, and he wasn't breathing. I dug the dirt out of his mouth and began to give him mouth-to-mouth resuscitation, his body still buried. He started coughing and crying.

My neighbor, who had heard me screaming from a quarter mile away, came running. He grabbed a sharp-shooter shovel and a pick and we dug Cole out. By the time we were able to pull him from the mound, the ambulance had made the fifteen-mile journey from Minden.

Cole was conscious. Miraculously, he was able to talk. I drove him to the hospital where doctors examined him from head to toe, just checking everything. They said he was fine. They said the only damage that could possibly happen was that he could develop pneumonia from dirt in his lungs.

A few hours later he was released and we took him home. As we passed by my mother's house, just down the road from the land I was clearing, Cole saw some of his cousins in the yard playing. He told me to stop the car, and he got out and went to play with the kids as if there wasn't anything wrong.

That evening I watched him closely, leaving his side only to push the debris into the pit and cover it up. That night I sat by his bed all night long with my hand on his chest. I was afraid he would stop breathing.

———∿∿∿———

We had just about recovered from that scare when Chase began vomiting and developed diarrhea. Judy took him to a pediatrician in Shreveport, who put him on some medication and told us to watch him very closely. After three or four days, Chase didn't seem to be getting any better. He still had diarrhea and was vomiting. He seemed terribly dehydrated. Judy called the doctor, who told her to bring Chase in so they could replace the fluids intravenously.

Being a registered nurse, Judy knew procedures, so she told the doctor that if he was just going to put in an IV to get fluids in him, she'd take him to the local hospital and spare the forty-five-mile drive.

The staff there tried to insert the IV but they couldn't find a vein, a normal problem with many two-year-olds but not one who was already a robust fifty-two pounds. Chase was so out of it that he didn't seem to mind that they kept sticking him.

All the time they were trying to find a vein they were also running other tests. It wasn't long before Dr. Koehler came and informed us that they had chartered a jet to come to the Minden Airport, pick up Chase and rush him to Ochsner Foundation Hospital in New Orleans. Calmly, he explained that Chase's kidneys had completely shut down. He was in renal failure, and Ochsner was the best place to treat him. Doctor Koehler cautioned us not to get our hopes too high; he wasn't sure that Chase would be alive when he got there.

They told us that only one parent would be allowed to fly on the plane with Chase. We decided Judy would go with Chase. I would drive.

I ran out of the hospital, hightailed it to the house and grabbed a few changes of clothes. Judy's brother, who was working for me at the time and staying with us, jumped in the car and we headed to New Orleans. I know this sounds crazy, but I drove 310 miles in three hours and fifteen minutes. I only stopped twice: once when a policeman clocked me for doing 125 miles per hour, and once to fill up with gas. I ruined the car, just destroyed the engine to where it never started again, but I got there an hour before my baby did.

The doctors immediately put Chase on dialysis and started running more complicated tests, which revealed that he had a disease called Hemolytic-Uremic Syndrome, a very rare disease. They treated four or five cases a year and seldom did the child live.

Ochsner is a very large hospital, and it was filled with the most amazing people. Even though Chase was two, they treated him in the Pediatric Intensive Care Unit (PICU), where most of the babies were newborns. Everybody there, the doctors, the nurses and the janitors, knew us by name. Chase's case was so rare.

Every so often a helicopter would come in. The PICU specialists would rush to the heliport, then rush back with this little baby who they would take straight into heart surgery. A few hours later they'd bring the baby back out and put him or her in the intensive care unit over by Chase, the little chest stapled together. These people were absolute miracle workers. They would take Chase, IV stands and everything, and wheel him down the hallway so he could watch the helicopters come in.

I stayed with Chase, sometimes eighteen hours a day, in the PICU. He wasn't allowed anything to drink so he constantly begged for water. His thirst was so intense that they had to strap him to keep him from chewing the IV tubes. They told us this was common. Chase begged me for something to drink until I finally said, "Son, if you keep begging Daddy for something to drink, then Daddy will have to get up and leave." I didn't leave for eighteen days.

Ten days into Chase's ordeal, and stressed to the limit, I asked one of his physicians, Dr. Bonas, if there was something positive he could give me, some hope that I could hang onto.

Dr. Bonas looked at me. "Well, Marc, I think we can rule out any brain damage," he said.

I didn't even know there was a chance of brain damage.

We made friends with probably six or eight couples during this time, sharing our ups and downs with them in the intensive care waiting room. Truth is, I lived with these people, slept there with them. Judy stayed at home, taking care of Cole and working. She came back down as often as she could. I stayed with Chase constantly.

This period was one of the most traumatic times of my life. I think if anyone doesn't appreciate their children, they need to go to Ochsner Foundation Hospital in New Orleans and sit in the intensive care waiting room to witness the pain and the fear that is so prevalent there. We literally just held each other up. We cried together. We prayed together. We were all scared to death.

It was heart wrenching. I think of all those babies, Chase is the only one who survived.

After three weeks they gave us permission to bring Chase back home with the stipulation he would stay on an extremely strict diet. He could have no protein and no sodium. By now Chase had dropped from fifty-two to about thirty pounds and had lost all the hair on the back of his head from lying in bed all that time. But he hadn't lost his hunger or his resourcefulness. When nobody was looking, he filched a bag of potato chips and ate them all. Can you imagine the sodium in a bag of potato chips? We saw the empty bag and were scared we were going to lose our baby.

Two weeks passed, and we brought him back for more tests. They injected some type of radioactive material to trace as it went through his system. Just the thought of radiation in my boy was enough to scare me to death. They informed us that he would probably end up needing dialysis every few days, and a kidney transplant wasn't yet out of the question.

They told us to come back again in a few weeks, that they would know more then. So we prayed and worried and beat ourselves up over what we might have done, what we didn't do. We could hardly take our eyes off of Chase. We went to the New

Orleans Zoo to get our minds off of what was ahead, and we had the time of our lives, all the while knowing that we were going to get terrible news when we went to the hospital.

The experts injected the radioactive material, ran their tests. They mulled over the results. Then Dr. Poncy and Dr. Bonas asked if they could meet with us in their office. Here it was. Knees shaking, hearts hurting and minds racing we entered the doctor's office. They asked us to take a seat. Judy and I just sat there and looked at one another.

The doctors talked in some medical terms, elaborating on their findings and explaining how they arrived at their conclusion.

Then they delivered it.

"We don't understand it," one of them finally said. "We can't find where Chase has ever been sick."

I had only one reply.

"Praise God," I said.

SEVEN

Dead Man's Talk

HUNTING HAD ALWAYS BEEN PART of my life, and I treasured the time I spent with my buddies at an isolated lease outside Minden.

During the day we'd sit high in stands and take turns trying to bag a big buck, or we'd hunt squirrels or whatever was in season. At night, the day's kill dressed and dinner finished, we'd kick back around a blazing campfire and shoot the bull.

The place wasn't anything fancy. We'd managed to get a concrete truck back there and pour a twenty-five-foot-square foundation, on which we put up a very rustic wood cabin. There were cabinets on one end and a set of French doors, which I'd salvaged from a fire job, that led to a wooden deck out back. We had a bricklayer come in and build us a fireplace at one end and a pit out on the deck where we could cook and grill.

We slept in an old construction trailer in which we'd crammed eight or ten bunk beds and whatever furniture we could find. Water came from a gravity-fed, thousand-gallon tank up on a wood frame. Out to one side we had a skinning rack so we could dress any game we took right there. We built a small corral for the four-wheelers, not to keep them from jumping out but to keep thieves from jumping in. The power came from a generator and some solar panels. There were some luxuries—air conditioning and a television—but mostly it was a place to get away.

It didn't look like much, but I'll tell you one of the greatest joys of being a father, one of the greatest tools for getting close to your children, originated right there at that hunting lease.

When the day's hunting was done, when the day's kills were dressed, when dinner was a memory and some of our number were enjoying a cold one, we sat around the campfire and talked. Now we were leveling our sights on quarry no less elusive that what we had hunted that day.

The truth, plain and unvarnished.

My friends Mike and Pat Woodard introduced a concept they'd picked up from a friend. They called it Dead Man's Talk, and simply put, it was a no-tell confession. The name came from the notion that it was like talking to a dead man. A dead man couldn't repeat what was said. It would not make him angry or stick in his craw. It wouldn't change an opinion or influence a friendship. It would be said, and it would disappear forever like a breath on a cold night.

Now these confessions didn't have to be anything big or scandalous. It didn't have to be something that we did or didn't do. It could just be something of which we were ashamed or secretly proud. Maybe it was something like winning a local chili cook-off using Alpo dog food and chili powder. I'm not saying that was a product of Dead Man's Talk, because in order to be part of those discussions you were bound by the rules. It could also be something as silly as putting a beer can on the local Baptist minister of music's car hood and hiding around the corner. Then addressing him by name as he picked up the can and snapping a picture of him when he looked up. Then threatening to send the picture to the local church board if he didn't feed us.

Now I'm not saying that was a product of Dead Man's Talk either. You understand I can't. What I will say is that I wish I'd taken two pictures because he cooked pretty well.

Along the way I came to realize this wasn't just a way to unburden or get a few laughs. By sharing these stories we opened up areas in our lives that we hadn't shared with anybody. Knowing something about a buddy that nobody else knows, not even his wife or parents or kids, brings you closer to him. You know you share something special.

It sounded to me like the perfect relationship between father and son.

Cole was seven and Chase was three when I introduced the concept of Dead Man's Talk to them. I explained it just the way Mike had explained it to us at the lease. I told them they could tell me anything. That could mean anything they were doing or thinking of doing, anything their friends were doing or thinking of doing. Whatever they told me would stay with me. No matter how much I might want to punish them for it, I couldn't. No matter how much I wanted to lecture them, I wouldn't. That didn't mean I wouldn't explain the consequences of their actions or intended actions, or remember it and maybe use it to shape what I would teach them or how I'd try to influence them later. But I made certain they understood that what they told me during Dead Man's Talk only I would ever hear.

I promised them that on my life.

Now don't get me wrong. This might sound easy enough, but over the years my boys have told me things that would inwardly make my blood boil. I didn't show it outwardly. That goes against every natural instinct a man has as a father. But I knew raising a child was something that happened over time. If something they told me in Dead Man's Talk later helped me steer them away from taking drugs or falling in with the wrong crowd, it was worth it. That was big, of course, but it wasn't the most important benefit. The most important thing was building trust. I knew it would only take one time where I acted on what they told me to destroy whatever we had built. Just one betrayal of confidence would ruin it all. Even hinting about the subject to another could wipe out years of work.

The first few times my boys and I declared Dead Man's Talk the topics were, in the grand scheme of things, pretty simple. I can't reveal them—there is no statute of limitations or degrees of sanctity on Dead Man's Talk—but suffice it to say they were more important to my boys than they were to me. Maybe it was a practical joke we'd played on Judy or some little innocent secret that boys have.

Still, it was an act of trust on their part, and I needed to show them it went both ways. Sometimes I would notice insecurity in Cole or Chase. I'd declare Dead Man's Talk. In hushed tones I'd explain to them that I didn't want anybody to know, but I had the same problems when I was their age. I'd make a big deal about keeping it secret. As far as the boys were concerned, they might as well have held the secret to the A-bomb. They loved it that I trusted them with such embarrassing confidences. I'd reinforce it by pulling them aside later and telling them that I really appreciated that nobody else knew.

Gradually the subjects grew more serious. The boys told me about things that happened at school that they knew would upset Judy. The told me about relationship problems with other kids. There were times I was hurt and scared by what I heard. I wondered if some things weren't worth breaking the trust. But most of the stuff had already happened. I asked myself, *Would I have been better off not knowing? Or am I better off being able to make a difference?* I believed the knowledge would help me be a more thoughtful and supportive parent. It would allow me to steer my boys away from pitfalls, instead of trying to rescue them after they'd fallen in.

You know you're in a strong and supportive position as a father when your children don't take the easy way out, even if offered. One day Cole and Chase misjudged their approach to a dock and damaged the Jet Ski I co-owned with my business partner Wanda Allen. Wanda's husband, Bobby, knew that the boys would be in for a whipping when I found out, so he suggested they just keep it amongst themselves. Bobby would get it fixed, and everything would blow over. "I have to tell him," Cole said to Bobby. "I tell Daddy everything." That's the power of Dead Man's Talk.

If you're concerned that Dead Man's Talk won't work with your relationship, if you think it's already too late for you and your loved one, remember that I was introduced to the concept when I was in my mid-thirties. It worked with my hunting buddies. It worked with my sons. It will work with anyone you want to build a better relationship with, no matter how reluctant they might be. The key is first showing the person trust. Tell the person a secret, not as if you're trying to see if you can trust him or her to keep it, but as if you're certain you can. Emphasize how important it is to you that the confidence to be kept, without threatening consequences if it isn't.

And remember, it only takes one violation of the Dead Man's Talk trust to ruin it forever.

—⁓—

Trust was the foundation of the relationship I wanted to build with my boys. I wanted them to trust me. And I wanted them to know that I trusted them even when they were angry with me, when they didn't think I knew a thing about what they were going through.

One day, when Cole was about to hit that difficult stage of a boy's life, we were driving down the old dirt road that passed my mother's house. He must have been eleven or twelve, and I knew some tough days were ahead.

We were holding hands as we drove, as we frequently did. Taking a hand off the steering wheel I pointed to my mother's home, a big white frame farmhouse.

"Son, you know a day will come when I will say to you, 'Isn't that a nice, pretty white house?' You are going to know in your heart and you are going to know in your head that the house is white. But for some reason or another you're going to say, 'Dad, that house is black.'

"I know you don't understand what I'm trying to tell you, son. But one day it doesn't matter what Dad says. Dad is going to be wrong. That is just the way you are going to feel. That's okay because it is something all young boys go through. It is called puberty. That day is coming."

He said, "No, Dad, that will never happen."

Three years later Cole and I clashed on something. I don't remember what it was, and that's not even important. I do know that it required discipline. I whipped Cole very hard and sent him to his room to give him a few minutes to think about what he'd done and the discipline he received.

Now you may think I'm cruel because I whip my children hard. But when I whip them, I whip them as if it's the last time. I don't ever want to have to whip them again. When I whip them, I feel it's my shortcomings as a father that are to blame for their actions.

When I discipline my kids, I don't sleep that night. This night was no different, so I was wide awake when a large shadow loomed over me. It was three o'clock in the morning. Cole leaned over and kissed me on the mouth. I could taste the big salty tears.

"Dad," he said, "today I was seeing that white house as being black, wasn't I?"

Then he turned and went back to his room. I laid there for what must have been fifteen minutes before I even remembered what we had talked about that afternoon three years earlier.

That moment I realized two things. I realized I'd reached where I wanted to be every time I striped their backsides with my belt. They hurt, but not from the whipping. In fact, Cole eventually wouldn't even flinch as I whipped him. Instead, he hurt inside. He would hurt so much inside he'd come to me to apologize for what he did to deserve the whipping.

I also realized that I never knew when and to what my children might be listening. I realized that I had to be careful what I said and how I said it.

I had learned early on that listening was important. When I was in third grade I was sitting around listing to my daddy talk to some people about eating oysters. I wasn't part of the conversation, but I listened nonetheless.

At school the next day we were swapping news about the events of the day before, as we always did. Someone talked about how they had gotten a hamster. I promptly told the class that my dad ate hamsters. They laughed at me and teased me to no end, trying to convince me that my dad did not eat hamsters. But that's what I'd heard. I would have bet my life on it.

That afternoon I went home from school and, in all my indignation, told my dad my classmates wouldn't believe me when I said he ate hamsters. Dad, suppressing a laugh, made me understand that it was oysters, not hamsters, that he ate raw.

I learned four lessons that day. I learned to listen. I learned that no matter how right you might think you are, no matter how cocksure you are, even to the point you'd bet your life on it, you could be wrong. I learned that being so convinced you're right when you're so wrong can be utterly humiliating.

I also learned never to order hamster at an oyster bar.

That reminds me of another story. Shortly after Cole died I was low and needed a boost. I needed to know I was a good father. I needed to know that my kids had learned from me, that I'd made a difference.

Off-handedly I asked Chase what he'd learned from Dad.

Chase fetched a pen and paper and started writing.

1. Don't let anyone steal your dream.
2. You can work now and play later, or you can play now and work later.
3. If it doesn't help you play football, don't do it. (drugs and drinking)
4. It doesn't matter what you can do, it matters what they think you can do.
5. Appearance is everything.
6. Sometimes your closest friends want to see you fail.
7. A young man will hurt you. An old man will kill you.
8. One-time things turn into lifelong addictions.
9. Sometimes being different is a cool thing to do.
10. When someone you love asks you to do them a favor, do it.

11. You don't tell someone you love them, you show them.

12. You never know how many people are watching you.

13. Sometimes just calling someone by their first name means so much to them.

14. Never cross your arms, put your hands over your package or anything that shows weakness when you're speaking to someone.

15. A handshake tells so much about a man.

16. Look everyone in the eye while you're talking to them.

17. Always walk like you're going somewhere.

18. Never, ever be late.

19. You will never know why parents act the way they do until you have kids of your own.

20. Also congratulate others on their accomplishments.

21. Treat the not-so-attractive girls just as good as the good-looking ones.

22. Don't put off until tomorrow what you can do right now.

Chase sat down and wrote these in five minutes. He told me he could write more if I wanted him to.

I still keep that folded paper in my wallet.

Dead Man's Talk wasn't the only way we built trust.

One day, when Cole was about nine, I was coaching him in City League basketball. We were playing a team with a big kid who was fairly aggressive. That's a nice way of saying he was dirty. He and Cole were guarding each other, and there was a lot of extracurricular pushing and shoving.

Eventually Cole had enough of it. When the kid pushed, he pushed back. The kid took a swing at Cole. Cole didn't start many fights but he never balked from finishing them. He hit the kid three or four times.

Because Cole was my son and I didn't want it to look bad, I jumped up, grabbed Cole and dragged him back to the bench, fussing at him the whole way. He didn't play the rest of the game.

Some of the other parents asked me why I overreacted. They said Cole was just defending himself. They told me I was wrong.

That stung, but what stung most was the look in Cole's eyes. He thought I should be encouraging him for standing up for himself, not humiliating him by grabbing and fussing at him in front of all those people.

Halfway through the drive home I pulled the car over and did something my Daddy never did. I looked him in the eye and said, "Son, today Daddy was wrong." I explained to him how I didn't want it to look like I was protecting my child, playing favorites. I told him I felt I had to be harder on him so that I wouldn't look like a parent defending his kid instead of an impartial coach.

I told him I was sorry and I would do anything to make it up to him.

At first I regretted doing that, but later I was glad it had happened. I've always been an advocate of finding something good from something bad. Something good came from that episode. Cole understood his father not only could make mistakes but also would admit them. That made us even closer. Cole Pittman was learning to trust me more.

With that trust came more and more sessions of Dead Man's Talk. Dead Man's Talk could happen at any time in any place. We could be sitting out on the back deck of our town house, or they could invite me into their bedroom. It could be in the truck as we drove somewhere or in a quiet corner at the gym. When Cole was in high school we'd often declare Dead Man's Talk as we ate our traditional Italian lunch at Monjunis restaurant on game days.

Judy respected our time. If she came home and saw Cole and me or Chase and me talking, she'd say, "Dead Man's Talk?" If it was, she'd leave us alone.

Dead Man's Talk isn't just something between a father and son. It can occur as well between a mother and her daughter, or a mother and her son, or a father and his daughter. It can happen between brothers or sisters or cousins or friends, any place where it can make a relationship tighter.

The day we buried Cole it was evident something else was bothering Chase. He came to me and declared Dead Man's Talk. He proceeded to tell me several things he'd done, things that would get many fathers' anger up in an instant.

I only nodded.

Chase asked me why I didn't show any emotion.

"Son," I told him, "I already knew all that."

Chase looked at me. Then his eyes lightened, and he broke into a smile.

"Cole," he said.

"Cole," I said.

And we had a good laugh.

EIGHT

The Bears We Wrestle

M Y DAD WAS ALWAYS LARGER than life to me. I guess I figured my dad could do anything.

When my boys were young I had an opportunity to try to create that kind of aura. A tavern about fifteen miles from the hunting lease was bringing in a wrestling bear. Right off, in no small part because of my reputation, I started getting phone calls inviting me to tussle with the bear. The owner even called.

I bit.

Now I might have been big and strong but I wasn't totally stupid, so I didn't tell Judy of my plans. I just got together with my buddies and headed to the tavern.

When we arrived the owner briefed the crowd on the rules. They were simple: Wrestle the bear for two minutes. Win and get one hundred bucks.

The first guy to take on the bear was about my size and weight, give or take the generous number of cocktails he had consumed to screw up his courage.

"Bring on the bear!" he kept screaming.

The owner obliged. Out came a brown bear, seven-and-a-half feet tall and 725 pounds. It wasn't all bad news. He was wearing a muzzle.

I began to think this fight was a no-win situation, but I figured it was worth my best shot. The Mouth of the South guy was going first, so I figured I'd go to school on him.

I did for all of ten seconds. By then the guy was flat on his back, the bear on top of him and the guy screaming for somebody to get the bear off him.

In another situation it would have been hilarious.

Now it was my turn. I figured I couldn't beat the bear fighting like a bear, so I told its trainer to make the bear stand up and fight me like a man.

He said, "Son, just walk up there close. She'll stand up."

That's the last time I listen to a bear trainer. When I walked up there close, that bear swatted me at the bend of the knees. My feet went toward the ceiling, my head toward the floor. That bear piled on, trying to flip me and pin me.

This wasn't like any street fight I'd ever been in. She kept trying to flip me, and I kept trying to stay on my belly. She was just clawing away. Finally, out of anger and frustration, I reached up inside the mask and grabbed the bear by the tongue. I wanted to pull that bear's tongue out.

She was bellowing, and I figured I was in good shape. Then I heard the disc jockey.

"Give her all you got, Pittman," he said. "You've got one more minute."

For one minute I squeezed a bear's tongue.

I have never been so winded in all my life as when they pulled that bear off of me. And that was the upside. They had cut the bear's claws, but they hadn't filed them smooth. I looked like I had been in the street fight of all street fights. When I got home that night around midnight, Judy saw the scratches on my face and welts on my body and asked what had happened.

I told her I had been wrestling a bear. She asked me, "Did you win?" I told her no. She laughed all night long. I was afraid I had gotten in trouble. If I had told her where I was going she would have fussed at me. But afterwards she was adamant that she had wanted someone to get the best of me for a long time. She would have paid good money to see that bear rough me up.

Nobody beat that bear and nobody won that money, but later I got a second chance to redeem myself.

The tavern owner brought in a second bear that wasn't as big. This one was only about six-foot-six and five hundred pounds. All the guys wanted to go back down there. I had had enough bear wrestling, so I wore some good clothes so they couldn't con me into wrestling the bear.

We watched as two or three other men wrestled the bear and got whipped. My good friends began to hassle me and prod me into wrestling the bear.

I pulled out all the stops.

I complained I had on boots and I would slip. They said get barefooted.

I complained I had a nice shirt on. Mike Woodard volunteered his cashmere sweater.

I was stuck.

This bear didn't have a muzzle because they had recently pulled all his canine teeth. And he was a younger bear that didn't have much knowledge of wrestling.

This was good.

The bear stood up, clamped his mouth over my neck and shoulders and we hugged. Mike's nice cashmere sweater must have aggravated the gums where they had pulled the bear's teeth because he bled all over that sweater.

Somehow I managed to get the bear on his back. That wasn't enough. You're supposed to be able to pin the bear, but the bear's shoulders are round. It's impossible to pin him. But I did keep him on his back and eventually, by popular vote of the bar's patrons, won the bear wrestling contest.

The prize was $100. The bar tab was $138.

That wasn't the only cost. Mike got in trouble the next morning as he was washing the blood out of the cashmere sweater in the utility room. His wife thought he might be washing makeup out of his sweater. He had trouble convincing her otherwise.

I came out slightly better. Not only would the boys be able to say that I wrestled the bear, they would be able to say I beat the bear.

We all wrestle bears in our life. They're not all seven feet tall and furry, but they can be just as imposing. It's how we deal with those bears that makes us who we are. And it's wrestling those bears in the right way, where our kids can see it and learn from it, that can generate the type of respect that makes their lives better.

—⁓—

Cole Pittman had a lot of things going for him. He was tall, strong, fast, very athletic and good-looking—and that's not all just a daddy talking. He scored most of the team's goals in soccer and was the starting center on the basketball team. He could dunk a basketball by the time he was in eighth grade. He had a great arm in baseball and was a natural in football. There wasn't a sport he tried where he didn't excel.

I'm a father, so indulge me a little bragging on my boy. He was a fearless kid who could drive, forward and reverse, just about any motorized vehicle by the time he was eight. He was eight when he took his first deer. When we'd fish he'd use topwater bait and hook a water moccasin, all spittin' and hissin', which he'd reel into the bottom of the boat. Grinning, he'd ask me if I would unhook his line and throw the snake overboard for him.

He was tough. I don't know if there's any physical pain that could make Cole Pittman cry. Maybe that's in the Pittman genes. Both my parents had high pain thresholds, and I was raised to be tough. Judy endured long labors to birth monster baby boys without the aid of an epidural or any painkillers. Whatever natural toughness he had, I made sure I built on.

When they were young I taught my sons the difference between physical pain and the pain you hold inside. One day when Chase was five I heard him standing in the yard screaming. He'd been stung by a wasp. When I got him to hush for a minute I told him, "Son, crying doesn't make it feel any better. You can cry if you want to, but you're just wasting a lot of tears and breath. That's physical pain. Physical pain isn't anything compared with the hurt that comes inside your heart. That's the pain that really hurts."

Chase wiped his eyes and nodded.

A week or so later we were coming back from church and stopped for groceries. Judy had gone in the store, and Cole and

Chase were strapped in the back seat. A wasp flew in the window. Chase caught it with his hand, stuck it out the window and let it go.

Cole acted like the older brother. "Chase, you're so stupid," he said. "That was a wasp. Didn't he sting you?"

Chase nodded. "Yeah, but it doesn't hurt," he said. "That's physical pain. Real pain is here." He patted his heart.

When Cole was in eighth grade at Glenbrook Christian Academy in Minden, there was an eleventh-grader who didn't like the attention Cole was getting. He decided he was going to make Cole's life miserable.

I could sense a change in Cole's demeanor. He became quieter and more serious. I could tell something was bothering him, but Cole kept silent. He usually talked to me about just about everything, but I think because of my reputation as a fighter and tough guy he was reluctant to talk about this, that he was afraid I might think he was wormy for not being able to handle this on his own.

After a while Cole finally confided in me about how the kid picked on him, but only when the kid was surrounded by his buddies.

What I told Cole must have been the last thing he wanted to hear.

"Son, you're going to have to let this kid know that you will fight," I said. "The next time this kid does anything to you, you hit him with all you've got. You hit him right on the end of the nose. You may get whipped, but people will find out you'll fight, that you'll defend yourself, and they'll leave you alone."

Well, that approach worked, but only for a while. Now the kid flipped him off and then hurried into the classroom.

"Would you like to end this once and for all?" I asked Cole.

"Yes, sir," Cole said.

I knew where the kid lived, so I told Cole, "Get in the vehicle." I turned and looked at Chase and I said, "Son, would you like to see Cole whip this boy?" Chase was always ready for a fight and certainly ready to witness one. "Yes, sir," he said. So he climbed in too. We went to the kid's house. On the way over there I coached Cole on fighting. "Get him down, don't let him up, and put him in the hospital."

If it had come down to it, I wouldn't truly have let Cole put him in the hospital. Or let the boy do the same to Cole. But I was certain it wouldn't get to that point. Growing up I had plenty of experience with this kid's type. From all the times I got beaten up by the bullies at my school, I knew those kind of kids were only tough when the numbers were on their side. And even if they did mix it up one-on-one, they'd get up and leave as soon as they started getting the best of you. They don't have the mentality to finish. All I needed was for Cole to convince the boy he didn't feel the same way.

In fact, I had Cole so pumped by the time we got there I think he believed he would put the kid in the hospital. I rang the door-bell and the kid's mother answered the door. I asked for the kid by name. She said he wasn't there and asked what was wrong. I said, "Well, Cole is here, and Cole is fixing to put him in the hos-pital. He has picked on Cole, he has done this, he has done that, and it's disrupting Cole at school, and this needs to be addressed."

She said, "Let me get my husband."

I also knew this guy very well; he was a deputy sheriff. I explained to him what happened. I told him that we were going to end it, where it was just Cole and this young man. I had informed Cole that I wanted him to beat him, beat him, beat him until he put him in the hospital. And that I would intervene if anybody else intervened.

The kid's dad said the boy wasn't there, but he would be in at a later time and he would bring him to our house. At ten thirty the doorbell rang. It was this man, his wife and his son. I brought them in and sat them down on the couch. I went and got Cole and sat him on the couch. I asked the kid why he was doing these things. He didn't have an answer.

I then asked him if he thought he could whip Cole, and he said he didn't know. I asked Cole if he thought he could whip him. Cole said, "Yes, sir."

Then I explained it to the kid. "You know, you're fixing to get your opportunity, but you need to understand, I have told Cole to put you in the hospital. I don't want him to stop until your eyes are blacked out, your nose is broke, and your teeth are gone. I want him to hurt you. You are going to have the same opportunity to hurt Cole, and we're not going to stop it."

The kid went to crying and begging. He didn't want to fight. This young man's daddy also starting crying. He apologized to Cole and explained to his son that he had embarrassed him and promised Cole that nothing like this would ever happen again. Then they left.

I'm not telling this story to enhance how tough Cole was, but instead I'm telling it because I think it is important that our kids know they will have to fight. Especially if it is to fight for what's right. If our kids allow people to push them around, it will become a way of life. It will eventually destroy the child's self-esteem. If you are not willing to fight, then you are going to get pushed around. If you are willing to fight, you are probably not going to have to.

NINE

Learning to Care

M Y BOYS HAD A LOT going for them. Most of all they knew how it was to love and to be loved.

Now you might be thinking that I thought my kids had everything, that they were perfect. They might have been perfect sons, but I knew they were far from being perfect people.

Growing up as Cole Pittman wasn't all touchdowns and game-winning baskets and glory. With those accomplishments came jealousy and insecurity. Even though I raised my sons not to be boastful, some people need to put others down to make themselves or their children look or feel better. I explained to Cole and Chase that this behavior is not uncommon. It's important not to listen too closely to criticism, not to be caught up too much in praise. The truth is, sometimes your best friends want to see you fail.

As Cole received more attention for his athletic accomplishments, he seemed to feel more pain. He was stung by jealousy, and his self-esteem—which he seemed to inherit from his daddy—often lagged.

Cole had a vain side, so right before football team pictures his junior year he decided he needed a little more color. He went to a tanning salon. He had just finished his session when he overheard a boy he knew talking to two girls in the next room. The girls were asking the kid about this boy named Cole Pittman. The kid, not knowing Cole was next door, referred to him as a joke, that he wasn't all he was cracked up to be.

Cole considered this kid a friend, so when he came out he pulled the kid to the side and asked him why he said those things about him. The kid said he was just joking. Cole knew he wasn't.

When Cole came by to discuss this with me, my heart ached for him. I could see he was deeply hurt, and I could see that Cole Pittman was beginning to have the same relationship problems I had had at his age. Cole was rapidly starting to dislike who he was. I knew, from personal experience, how that could become a habit.

I told him the only thing I could possibly think to tell him. It just so happened to be the truth.

Of all the people in the world, I told him, if I could be any-body it would be Cole Pittman. He was athletic, good-looking, talented and had the whole world out there in front of him. Cole Pittman didn't need to allow people to make him dislike himself.

You're probably wondering how I can put this in writing when I have another son. The reason is that I was eventually able to say the same thing to Chase.

—∿—

I not only wanted to protect my boys from the cruelty of others; I wanted to make sure they never acted that way them-selves. It's called compassion, and in many ways it's the true measure of a man.

When Cole was about nine years old he got into a fight at church. He was attending a meeting of Royal Ambassadors for Christ, a Christian youth group, when two boys started picking on a smaller boy. Cole stood up for him.

I didn't know this when I arrived to pick him up, but it didn't take long to find out. Even before I walked through the doors, a lady jumped all over me, telling me Cole was fighting in church and I should be ashamed.

Not knowing the reason for his fisticuffs, I *was* ashamed. I asked Cole what had happened, and he told me about the two boys picking on the smaller boy and how he had whipped them both.

I told him he wouldn't be getting a whipping, because what he did was commendable, sticking up for someone too weak to defend himself. He had done the right thing. But that didn't mean I was happy with his actions, and I told him why.

The lady didn't know why he was fighting. She just knew he was fighting. In her eyes he was the troublemaker.

Sometimes lessons don't come in black and white. Sometimes doing good comes with a bigger price than doing bad—or doing nothing at all. Cole decided that he'd take the chance of a whipping from me to protect someone. He'd take a whipping to prevent someone else from taking a whipping.

The lessons, and Cole's sense of right, wouldn't stop there.

One afternoon, in Cole's junior year, he showed up after football practice with a teammate, a little black running back named Jeff Duncantale. Cole said that Jeff didn't have a place to go that night, so he told him he could stay with us. Our townhouse was pretty small, only about twelve hundred square feet, so I had turned the garage into a third bedroom, where Cole slept. Cole told Jeff he could stay there with him.

Now, I was raised in a segregated community and taught that blacks and whites ought not to mix. But I thought I could put up with Jeff staying over for a night. The next day Jeff came home with Cole again, and the next day after that. Two weeks went by, and I called Jeff into the room. Looking him straight in the eye I told him that I'd house him, feed him and take care of him, but that he would have to follow the house rules.

Jeff just hugged me and kissed me.

Cole had been around me too much already, and he knew how I was. He was just sitting back and seeing how Dad was going to react. He didn't care about the color of Jeff's skin or anything else; he would give the shirt off his back to anybody. He wanted to see what I would do.

The real test came when we went to my mother's house to have Thanksgiving with my family.

I had sense enough to warn my mother that I would be bringing an extra mouth to feed, but I don't recall if I said the extra mouth would be a black kid. I walked in first and backed up to the fireplace. Cole and Jeff followed me in.

My older brother looked at Jeff. "What the hell was that?" he asked me, as if Jeff wasn't even there.

"That is Cole's friend and that's my friend, and he is going to be here for Thanksgiving lunch," I said. "Do you have a problem with that?"

He was quick to reply. "Yes I do."

There was no doubt in my mind that I could whip my brother. He was considerably older, and I was in pretty good shape, but I'd moved beyond that stage in my life. Momma didn't say anything, but I could tell by the look in her eye that she was pleading with me not to start any trouble, that we just needed to leave.

Cole, Jeff and I went outside and gathered around the truck.

"Boys, it looks like we're not welcome here," I said. "I will feed you Thanksgiving lunch anywhere you name."

Cole looked over at Jeff.

"You got any particular place in mind?" he asked.

Jeff just shook his head. I could tell he couldn't believe what had just happened.

Cole had an idea. He broke into a sly smile.

"If it's my choice, I think we need to have lunch on Rayville's football field right at the fifty-yard line," he said.

Evangel was set to play at Rayville the next night in the state play-offs. Rayville was 150 miles to the east. Rayville it was. While we had been figuring out what to do, some of my sisters packed up a nice Thanksgiving lunch in a basket, with everything from turkey to pie. We packed it in the truck and headed to Rayville.

We spread our blanket on the fifty-yard line, and we ate Thanksgiving lunch.

As a contractor I always kept a Polaroid camera in the truck. Cole went and got it and had me take a photo of him and Jeff, sitting at midfield and smiling at the camera. He took a piece of paper and wrote a short note and put it and the picture on the home team's bench.

The note read, "Today we ate the stuffing out of our turkey, tomorrow we'll beat the stuffing out of you."

Standing up for Jeff made me grow bigger than life in Cole Pittman's eyes. He was so proud of his dad, how I didn't back down to my family. And I can hardly describe how proud it made me of Cole. He knew how I was raised, and he wanted to make sure that what I'd been telling him about how to treat people, all people, wasn't just empty talk. And I was proud he was judging people on who they are, not what they are.

I know the way my brother acted was wrong, but please don't beat him up over that. It hadn't been that long since Marc Pittman would have done the same thing. The difference was that he didn't have Cole Pittman to help change his life.

You might be wondering what happened to Jeff. He stayed with us for a few weeks after football, but one day he left and never came back. About a week after Cole's death, the doorbell rang. I went to the door and there was Jeff, tears streaming down his face and his eyes big as saucers.

I didn't say a word. I just turned and walked to the bedroom. He followed me.

There I handed him a large portrait of the University of Texas tower with a number forty-four lit up on the side. I handed him a picture of Cole and his University of Texas football helmet. He took each thing and held it close to him, tears rolling down his face. "Chase is upstairs," I told him.

Jeff went upstairs. I left the house for a few minutes to take care of some business. When I came back, Jeff was gone. I haven't seen him since.

TEN

Love Wars

EVERY FATHER IS GOING TO fight battles with his son. There's no way around it. That's what being a good father is all about. You just have to fight the right ones in the right way.

For the last fifteen years I've fought a war I didn't want to lose but couldn't stand to win.

The war's rules of engagement are simple. I try to outdo my sons. My sons try to outdo me.

The weapon is love, and the battlefield is our hearts.

We call them Love Wars.

We came up with that name when Cole was in high school at Evangel Christian Academy in Shreveport, but in truth we'd been exchanging salvos since he was just a small child.

Whatever we could do to show the other that we loved him more, we did.

When we scored a hit it was like an unspoken "gotcha."

Some hits were small. An "I love you" was returned with an "I love you more." A hug was answered with a kiss. Sometimes my boy would call me five times a day just to say, "Dad, I love you so much."

Some hits were bigger. When Cole was a freshman at Texas he lost in the sandpit where the players worked on their leg strength the gold number-forty-four necklace I'd given him. I drove the ten-hour round trip, rented a metal detector and we found it.

Gotcha.

Waiting for Cole one day outside the football complex, I was talking to one of his teammates.

"You're larger than life around here," the player said.

"I ain't done anything," I said.

"Tell that to Cole."

Gotcha.

Looking back, I guess the Love Wars started in earnest when Cole was playing Dixie Baseball. He was only nine, but because of his size he played up, on a team with eleven-year-olds.

One day I had to work late and arrived at the game after it started. It was already the first inning, but Cole was standing outside the fence of the dugout as his team batted. I walked up to the fence, leaned over and kissed him on the mouth. We had done this from a very young age, and I didn't think anything about it.

On the way home, he asked me. "Dad, how come I never see any of the other boys kiss their dads?"

I was quiet for a minute. Then I said the first thing that came to mind.

"I guess they don't love their daddies as much as you do," I said.

It was like a light went off in that boy's eyes. From that day on, Cole Pittman made it a point to kiss me. Even at twenty-one years of age, in front of eighty-three thousand fans, Cole Pittman kissed me on the mouth.

I'm six-foot-six, about 268 pounds. Cole was six-four and 295 pounds the day he died. When two men kiss each other or hold hands in public, as we often did, there is often a negative reaction. In our case it was just the opposite.

When Cole was in the eighth grade, he was starting for Glenbrook Christian Academy in Minden. Cole was probably the second biggest player on the team, one that went undefeated in the regular season but lost in the play-offs.

When I walked into the gym for a pep rally Cole kissed me on the mouth.

The biggest kid on the team, a rough-cut senior, was taken aback.

"Cole, you still kiss your daddy?"

Cole turned to him.

"Yes, I kiss my daddy. Don't you ever kiss your daddy?"

"No, I don't kiss my daddy, and if I did, I wouldn't kiss him on the mouth."

Cole surprised me again. "What's the matter, don't you love your daddy?"

The kid was defiant. "Yeah, I love my daddy."

"Then kiss him so he will know it."

"Maybe I will," the kid said.

Sometimes I worried that the affection was maybe too much. Maybe I was wrong. My daddy never kissed me. When Cole was probably eleven or twelve years old, when I was just starting out as a contractor, I was out doing an estimate on a potential job at a lady's house. She was holding a book, and to make a little conversation I asked her what she was reading.

She named a book by some child therapist, but I don't recall the title of the book or the author's name.

"Do you know what this guy says?" she said.

"What does he say?"

"He says the reason there are so many male homosexuals in this world is because little boys get up to be four or five years old and their dad starts pushing them away. They shake their hands and tell them to be a man. These kids grow up looking for male affection."

I knew my boys were not going to grow up looking for male affection. They could get all the male affection they wanted from their dad.

That idea is the basis of Love Wars, and this is one battle I don't want to win but can't stand to lose. As a parent I tried not to focus on how much my kids loved me but on how much I could love them. If I could show them my love was unconditional—that they could always trust me implicitly and that I would admit when I was wrong—in my heart I knew I couldn't lose.

Cost didn't matter—not financial cost or cost in time or convenience or bother. If love doesn't cost much it's probably not worth much, anyway.

After the spring game during Cole's freshman year at Texas the players were lined up at tables for an autograph session. I was standing nearby when a man in his early thirties approached me.

"Mr. Pittman, Mr. Pittman. I need to talk with you," he said. "Do you have any idea how special your son is?"

I was proud but humble.

"Yes, sir, I do," I said. "He's a pretty special young man."

The man shook his head.

"I don't think you understand what I'm saying. Do you have any idea how special your son is?"

"Sure I do. He's my son. I think he's special."

"I don't think you understand. Let me tell you what Cole did."

The man proceeded to tell me how he had taken his five-year-old son to a spring scrimmage. After the workout the boy approached Cole, who was talking with several teammates and a few adults, and tugged on his jersey.

Cole stopped the conversation. He stooped down and asked the boy what he was going to do when he grew up, what his name was, what school he went to. Cole spent fifteen minutes with the boy, the man said.

By now the man had tears rolling down his face.

"Mr. Pittman," he said, "people don't do that anymore. Your son is special."

Cole was becoming the man I'd hoped he'd be. He'd scored a "gotcha" without even knowing it.

Each "gotcha" didn't always hit its mark right away. Sometimes it took years, but that only made it more on target.

The last time I had drunk anything of significance was the night before I got married. You remember I was beat up pretty badly, and I had sense enough not to get drunk again. I had an occasional beer with my buddies, but most of the time I was the designated driver when we went out.

On this particular day we were building deer stands. Being a contractor and being very good with my hands, I was doing the bulk of the work. We had food on the grill, and we were having a good time. And I was building up a thirst.

By lunchtime I had all but one stand built and I needed a cold one. There was no drinking water but there was a huge iced chest of beer. But I knew that every time I drank a beer, I became lazy. So when we stopped and ate, I didn't drink a beer. No big deal, no life-changing decision there.

I was sitting there, finishing my lunch and watching a football game on a small television we'd rigged to the generator, when Chase came up to me. He couldn't have been more than seven or eight at the time. He leaned in and whispered in my ear.

"Dad, thanks for not drinking a beer," he said.

You think I wanted a beer then?

We finished our stands and set out on the drive home, with Chase in the back seat and Cole in the front seat. The camp house was still in my rearview mirror when Cole spoke.

"Dad, I noticed you didn't drink a beer today," he said.

Now I'm no genius, but I figured this was pretty special to my boys.

"Hey guys, I didn't realize it was that important to you," I told them. "I'll never drink another one."

They'd scored a direct hit, Love Wars–style.

My return was on target, too. I haven't had a beer to this day.

It wasn't until years later, after Cole had gone to college and the nightlife and partying that goes on at any school, that I realized how important this was. Cole wasn't a drinker, but that didn't mean it wasn't going on all around him and that he wasn't tempted. Some football players would later tell me they had

READER/CUSTOMER CARE SURVEY

HEMG

We care about your opinions! Please take a moment to fill out our online Reader Survey at **http://survey.hcibooks.com**. As a **"THANK YOU"** you will receive a **VALUABLE INSTANT COUPON** towards future book purchases as well as a **SPECIAL GIFT** available only online! Or, you may mail this card back to us.

First Name		MI.	Last Name	
Address				City
State		Zip		Email

1. Gender
□ Female   □ Male

2. Age
□ 8 or younger
□ 9-12   □ 13-16
□ 17-20   □ 21-30
□ 31+

3. Did you receive this book as a gift?
□ Yes   □ No

4. Annual Household Income
□ under $25,000
□ $25,000 - $34,999
□ $35,000 - $49,999
□ $50,000 - $74,999
□ over $75,000

5. What are the ages of the children living in your house?
□ 0 - 14   □ 15+

6. Marital Status
□ Single
□ Married
□ Divorced
□ Widowed

Comments _____

_____
_____
_____
_____
_____

BUSINESS REPLY MAIL

FIRST-CLASS MAIL PERMIT NO 45 DEERFIELD BEACH, FL

POSTAGE WILL BE PAID BY ADDRESSEE

Health Communications, Inc.
3201 SW 15th Street
Deerfield Beach FL 33442-9875

made a big deal out of Cole not drinking. They encouraged him to drink, just to have a beer with the guys.

One night Cole and I were talking on the phone.

"You know, Dad, I understand now," he said. "When you were drinking a beer with the guys, you weren't getting drunk. You were just having a beer with the guys. I guess there wasn't anything wrong with it."

Boy, was I ready for this. I was all but giggling.

"No, it wasn't a big deal, Son, but it was important to you, so I didn't do it. Now you're down there at the University of Texas, you're with your friends and all of a sudden it's not that important to you anymore. But you know what? It's important to me now. I loved you enough to stop, how much do you love me?"

Man, I was glad I didn't drink beer anymore. I could just picture old Cole squirming. I knew he was grinning because I sure was. I had him on this one.

I think we have to understand as parents that this carries over not only to the drinking, but smoking or any bad habits we may have acquired. If we don't want our children to do them later on, we don't need to be doing them now. Fortunately, probably because I didn't have a way to go out, I never did much of anything in high school. I never had the opportunity to do these things, but I don't think I would have done them anyway because I was so crazy about my daddy. I was able to tell my kids that I didn't drink when I was in high school, I didn't smoke, I really didn't even cuss. I didn't do those things until after my daddy died.

I figured all I had to do now to keep my boys straight was to just stay alive.

ELEVEN

Learning to Let Go

I HAD HUGGED MY SONS most of their lives, pulling them close to me as if I never was going to let them go. But I knew the day would come when I'd have to let go, when they'd pick a college and go off to make their own way in the world.

That day was coming. It was fall 1998, and Cole had grown into a defensive line prospect that major colleges wanted to sign. Cole faced the difficult task of deciding which offer he would take.

The plan was for Cole to graduate in December after an All-American season at defensive end and go to college in January, so he could go through spring practice and get a head start on the other freshmen, who wouldn't be arriving until August. It was a busy time for the Pittmans. Every weekend it seemed we were going to some major university, so Cole could look at schools and decide where he was going to go.

This choice was the biggest decision my child would ever make in his life, and I was determined he would make it alone. I might point out certain things that I did and did not like about a school, but I was very careful not to show any partiality. I wanted this to be Cole's decision. If he made the wrong decision, I didn't want it to be because I had influenced him. My child being happy was the most important thing to me. I even designed a chart for him so he could evaluate and grade each college. I took into consideration time, distance, weather, coaching staff, stability of coaching staff, win-loss record—anything and everything that had to do with going to that university and playing football. He could grade each one, and at the end the one with the most points was where he needed to go.

Cole didn't really need the chart. He kept saying that when he found the right university, he would know it.

There was one university he had no interest in at all. But one day I was out working, and on three separate occasions someone approached me and asked if I'd looked at that same school: Texas.

Texas wasn't on Cole's list. He had no interest in the University of Texas. But after being asked that on three different times, twice by people who were graduates of our own state university, I was wondering what was going on.

When I returned to the house, the telephone rang. It was Evangel Coach Dennis Dunn.

"Marc, I just got off the phone with the University of Texas. They want to know if there is any way at all that you would come take a look?"

We had booked all our weekends with trips to universities, and the only open weekend was the one coming up. Cole was then dating a very beautiful young lady who was three years older than him, and they had made plans to go back to Louisiana State that weekend.

I called him downstairs.

"Son, Coach Dunn was just on the phone. He said Texas had called, and they want to know if there was any way that you would go and look. Son, that is the fourth time today that somebody has said something about Texas. I know you have plans to go to LSU, but wouldn't it be a shame to look back after you've traveled the road and say, 'Gosh, if I had only taken a look'?"

Cole had a way of getting to the point.

"Well, let's go to Texas," he said.

Over the years I have been on recruiting visits with a number of kids to numerous universities. The most important thing is that the child will be happy. In order for that to happen, you have to trust the people who will be taking care of him. So I was going to form an opinion and do some evaluations. I just wasn't going to allow Cole to know it.

We drove to Texas for an unofficial look around. I have been around some great head coaches and some great recruiters, but never in my life have I ever experienced anyone like Mack Brown.

I remember the first thing he said to Cole.

"Son, I'm not just recruiting great football players, I'm recruiting great football players with character. It doesn't matter how good you are. If you don't have character, I don't need you at Texas."

If you had asked Cole what his daddy's greatest ability was, he would say it was his ability to read people. I'm going to tell you, Mack Brown was not only saying the right things, he was as genuine as anyone I had ever experienced in my life. But it wasn't just Mack Brown. The football players, the fans . . . it was just like one great big family, very similar to Evangel.

When I compare a place to Evangel, that's the ultimate compliment.

I know Cole struggled with relationships at Evangel and even on some issues with the coaches, but I think that would have happened anywhere. It doesn't matter. For me and my boys, Evangel is holy ground. After our kids started going there, I even picked up a rock I found on the football field and carried it in my pocket for three years. I just wanted to have a piece of Evangel with me all the time.

Cole had already taken his official visit to Louisiana State, and he was going to go ahead and officially visit Texas, Florida and Nebraska. Those schools were his Final Four.

"I'm going to look at these schools just so I can be sure," he said. "Besides, right now, everyone is treating me like a king. I know that once I get to that university and I have signed on the dotted line, I'll be just another piece of meat."

He took all three visits in one week. It was the Christmas holidays. He had only one or two tests to take during the first week of January, and he would be ready for college. After his last visit, he came in, kissed me and flopped down beside me.

"What do you think?" he said.

"I think you have a pretty tough decision to make. You best be thinking on it."

"You're not going to help me on this one?"

"Son, I can't. This is the first of many important decisions you're going to have to make in life. These decisions will determine the person you will be."

Cole grinned.

"Dad, are you telling me I'm going to have to grow up?"

"Son, it took me forty-plus years to grow up. You are going to have to do it a lot quicker."

I told him to sleep on it and pray about it. I would not always be around, but God would always be there to help him make the tough decisions. The next night I was lying on the bed. He came in and closed the door behind him, crawled upon the bed and snuggled up next to me.

"Dad, I know where I'm going to school."

"That's good, Son, especially since you've only got a week to get ready."

He knew I was trying to make light of it. He also knew the very idea of my big boy going off to college was terrorizing me. My sons would come and kiss me a number of times during the day. The idea of him not being there to kiss me goodnight was something I really didn't want to think about.

"Dad, don't you want to know where I'm going to school?"

My heart was about to beat out of my chest, and I felt sure he could sense the anticipation, but I kept my voice level.

"Son, Dad trusts you to make all the right decisions. You can tell me now, or you can tell me when you announce it in church." Our top athletes typically announced the school of their choice in church. Cole would be doing the same.

"If it's all the same to you, I would like to go ahead and tell you."

"Let her rip," I said.

"I'm going to Texas."

I don't know if it was the look in my eye or just my inability to fool my boy. He followed up with another statement that shocked me. "Aren't you glad we both love the same place?"

Cole then asked me if I thought Mama could keep it under wraps until the announcement if we let her in on the news. We decided we would give it a try. The decision was exceptionally good news to Judy. She was a big-time LSU supporter and had a brother who had played for LSU. A couple of weeks earlier, though, she had been on a business trip to Austin and had an opportunity to go by Texas and get a taste of Mack Brown. When she returned from Austin, Judy told me, "I've never met anybody in my life who I would be more comfortable with leading my children." She wasn't just talking about athletics. She was talking about taking her oldest son to the next phase of his life.

Cole then called the other three schools—LSU, Florida and Nebraska—talked to the coaches who recruited him and told them he would not be coming, that he was going to Texas. For Cole it was the hardest part of the recruiting process. These coaches had spent a lot of time and money. He was aware of that. He had also developed close relationships with these people. I was in awe as I listened to his conversations. I was also sympathetic as I saw a tear roll down his face after one conversation with one particular coach. I was so proud of him.

—∿∿—

School would start in Texas in the middle of January. I had less than two weeks to prepare myself for what I knew was going to be very painful. I knew that when Cole went to college, the world would come after him. I wasn't going to give up easily. I solicited the best help I could find. I went and bought him a new Bible.

Inside the front cover I wrote an inscription.

> *My Son, My Son, My Son.*
>
> *Remember the blessing and the curse. The mind is the limit. As long as the mind can envision the fact that you can do something, you can do it, as long as you believe it 100 percent. I challenge you to keep this book where it is the last thing you see when you go to bed and the first thing you see when you get up. The key to your success is found inside this book.*
>
> *Read it, live it, don't let anyone steal your dreams. Remember, it's not where we start, it's how we finish.*
>
> *Love,*
> *Dad*

The blessing and the curse are from a story in the Bible in which people received great blessings if they followed God's command. The curse was seeing somebody else receive the blessing if they didn't follow God's command.

I also knew that if I asked Cole to commit to reading God's word every day, and he told me he would do it, he wouldn't let me down. I smiled as I gave Cole this Bible. I knew I was going to win this battle.

What I found out was that I had taught Cole too well in the art of Love Wars. Not only would I lose this battle; eventually I would lose the war.

Cole countered, giving me a Bible. On the first blank page he had written a poem. The poem is titled "To Be Because."

This Bible to the best Dad there ever was
You are the best Dad ever to be because
Because of the way you were my Father
You are a father like no other
Because we have something special,
Something no other father and son share
I do not dream of breaking it, I do not, do not dare
Because you were always standing by my side
Showing me to stand up for myself, never to run and hide
Because of the way we spent time together for our special talks
It never consisted of hollering and yelling,
But more like simple walks
Because no matter what, you always had the time
You never were aggravated, but attentive and kind

Because of the way you spoiled me, like a little brat
You got me all I ever wanted, I can't ask for more than that
Because of that, one day when I'm a father on my own
And I'll come to you and ask for advice of my own
Thank you Dad, for being the best Dad there ever was
You are the best Dad ever to be because.

The following week we packed the car with what Cole would need for school. Chase and Cole got in his truck, and Judy and I followed in our vehicle. It was a four-and-a-half-hour drive to Austin and I dreaded every mile, because I knew that once we arrived we would be leaving our son behind.

I tell you, my heart was so heavy I felt like I was dragging it behind me. Mama wanted his dorm room perfect. She had color coordinated and planned everything. It had to be her way. We humored her and let her set things up. It would be the last time that room would have any order at all. After that we went out and ate and headed back to the dorm for what would be good-bye.

Chase was handling it pretty well. He just kissed his brother and popped him with his fist and said, "See ya," and walked out the door. Judy took a little longer. She kissed him, she loved on him and made him promise if he needed anything to call her. Head hanging, she left, leaving just me and Cole standing there. She knew that we would need this time alone.

We stood there and looked at each other for what seemed like an eternity. Cole with that smile on his face, and me with that lump in my throat. I kissed him and then I whispered in his ear, "Pittman is your name now, Son. What are you going to do with it?"

I walked out the door, pulled it closed behind me and didn't look back.

TWELVE

Every Child Is Different

ON A SCALE FROM ONE to ten, my relationship with Cole would have been a ten. At that time my relationship with Chase probably would have been a five or six. By any measure, that's just average. Part of that was Chase's ability to have friends. He didn't need me as much as Cole, who shared my problems with relationships.

While Cole struggled, Chase was like the Pied Piper. While Chase had plenty of good relationships, Cole was like me, a boy who struggled and always felt inadequate and insecure. Cole and I became closer as a result of that bond.

Chase wasn't jealous. At least he never showed it. But Chase was always pretty good about hiding disappointment.

Right before Cole had turned fifteen I bought him a pickup truck for Christmas, so he could drive himself and his brother to school. Now, Louisiana law wound up helping me out when the legal driving age went up to sixteen, so I had an extra year to prepare for Chase to drive. The last Christmas before Cole was to go off to college, I got Chase a vehicle.

I could not possibly treat those boys differently, so I went and got Chase a new Montero Sport and hid it in the warehouse at the office. My neighbor and friend, Gerry Woolman, is an ordained minister and part-time preacher. He came up with idea to play a joke on Chase. I went along.

Gerry worked for a local dealership in town, and he wanted me to give Chase a ragged-out car and convince him that was his Christmas present. The stage was set, because I was telling Chase that I couldn't afford to buy him a vehicle.

Christmas morning we opened all our gifts, and the last thing we did was retrieve an envelope from the tree that had Chase's name on it. I think Chase knew immediately that it had a set of keys in it. When he opened it, he couldn't help but express his joy. It was then that I began to prepare him.

"Son, don't expect too much. You're going to need a way to get back and forth to school with Cole going away to college. We just did the best that we could. Later on we will do better."

Chase couldn't hide his excitement as he raced to the garage, opened the garage door and stood there in disbelief.

There sat a 1980 Chrysler LeBaron, platinum gray. That sounds better than primer gray, which it was. You had to be pretty strong just to be able to close the door. The vinyl dash had hardened and cracked, and the liner for the interior roof was actually a burgundy colored sheet that had been stapled or screwed to the top of the car. Foam was visible through slits and cracks all over the seats.

Chase just smiled and said, "Thank you."

With Cole standing there in shocked disbelief and Chase smiling, I said, "Well, let's just all take a ride."

The whole family piled into the car. When Chase started it, we had to wait five minutes for the smoke to clear so he could see enough to back out of the garage. The power steering was so bad that Cole had to get out and move another car so Chase could make the turn to get out of the garage.

I told them to head for my office. As I'd done with Cole, I'd established a contract for Chase to sign, stating rules the kids would have to abide by to keep their vehicle.

On the way to the office, the car, which had a computerized voice mechanism, proceeded to tell Chase he was low on fuel. Judy had a field day with this. "This car will actually talk to you," she said. "You ought to never run out of gas."

Judy was telling him that we could do some things to fix it up. We could get him some chrome rims for his birthday. Maybe even some seat covers to cover up his seats. Maybe even do the fuzzy dash that you see on some cars.

Chase started laughing.

"What's so funny?" I asked him.

He told us that one of his teammates, Thomas Bachman, also had a Chrysler LeBaron, though it was a much newer model. One of Thomas's hubcaps was missing, and Chase had picked at him about it.

"I sure wish I hadn't picked at Thomas about that hubcap," Chase said.

When we reached the office, the contract was lying on my desk. Without hesitation Chase walked over and signed that contract.

I was in absolute bewilderment. No kid could be this strong. As we were getting ready to leave, I told Cole and Chase that Mother had some Christmas boxes in the rear bay of the office that they needed to load in the car.

When they opened the door there was the Montero Sport, sitting there with a big red bow that read "Merry Christmas."

Chase just stood there and wept.

Later on I reflected on Chase's ability to conceal what had to be considerable disappointment when we gave him the ragged-out car. I think maybe Chase was willing to let Cole be the focus of our lives while he just stayed in the shadow.

In my mind, that was the furthest thing from the truth. I loved my boys equally. But I had to make sure Chase understood that, too.

I spent the next year trying to find a common denominator that would allow Chase and me to build a unique relationship, but he wasn't responding. He had developed some friends that weren't bad kids; they just weren't good kids. As a result he was doing some things that he shouldn't have been doing. I knew about these things, but could not say anything. Cole had told me all of it in Dead Man's Talk. I was thankful that Chase and Cole had developed such a close relationship.

This was Chase's sophomore year at Evangel. He had moved to the defensive side of the ball and was playing end, the same position Cole had played. I was afraid this would add even more pressure on Chase to compete with Cole. That never happened, if only because Chase dislocated his shoulder and only played about half the games.

I've always tried to find the good in something bad, and now I felt I finally had the common denominator that I had been searching for so diligently. I told Chase that the shoulder injury was going to continue to give him problems and he might not be able to participate in sports at all. I suggested we needed to starting hitting the weight room together.

Now I'm horrible on dates. I have to struggle to remember my own birthday most of the time. But I'll always remember January 5, 1999, the date my relationship with my younger son changed for the better.

Chase and I were in my truck, driving to the health club. We were on the Cross Lake Bridge, a two-mile span about a half-mile from our house.

I started by talking about my relationship with his brother.

"Son, Cole and I have an extraordinary relationship, and I want you to understand I will not apologize for that. But if you think that I love Cole more than I love you, nothing could be further from the truth. I love you both the same. The difference is that relationships are developed, they don't just happen. Cole was willing to put a lot more into a relationship with me than you have.

"I am going to put just as much into our relationship. We can have just as good a relationship or an even better relationship than Cole and I have. It depends on what you are willing to put into the relationship."

I knew the key to Chase and me developing a unique bond was the amount of time we spent together. So I took a chance and asked him a question.

"Son, how would you like to be one of the best-looking athletes in America?" Chase didn't say anything. "How would you like to be one of the strongest kids in America?" Silence again.

"This can happen, and it will happen to you, but only if you are willing to listen."

Things began to happen almost immediately. Not only was our relationship starting to develop, but Chase's strength and his physical appearance began to change noticeably. Humbly, I think God was helping me out on this, because after four weeks Chase had picked up about twelve pounds. Understand, we were eating six to seven meals a day, a lot of which were peanut butter and honey sandwiches. Chase was working out three times a week at Evangel and six times a week with me. He was really giving it all he had. But I wasn't done yet.

As we were crossing the bridge another day on our way to the gym, I noticed Chase was really dragging. I decided to push some buttons.

I got angry.

"Are you on drugs? What's the deal? You look absolutely horrible."

He told me he had been up all night with his friends playing cards. Angrily, he asked me never again to question if he was on drugs.

Now, I liked his response, and I could see the fire in his eyes. I especially liked the part about not questioning him about drugs. There was no doubt in my mind that he was not taking drugs.

But I didn't let up.

Sleep is critical, I told him. You have to establish patterns, eating habits, sleeping habits. To change those would make you lose weight. I took a chance and bet him that when we arrived at the gym and stepped on the scale he'd have lost seven pounds and that it would take him two weeks to get back what he lost.

I was wrong. He had lost nine pounds, and it took us three weeks to get it back.

I can't say I was unhappy about that. Now maybe my boy would realize Dad knew what he was talking about. Chase responded just as I'd hoped he would. He began to listen to me more and more. The more he listened, the closer we got.

One of my greatest friends is Ken Meeks, who owned The Plex, where we worked out. He's always been there for me, as a workout partner and an informal advisor on raising kids. Ken had raised a son and daughter, and many times we'd get in serious and intimate discussions about our children.

In this case, Ken wasn't making it easy on me. While the three of us were working out together, he always referred to Cole as "The Chosen One." Right off it frustrated me, because I figured I'd have enough problems developing my relationship with Chase. But a funny thing happened. Any time Ken used that phrase, I squirmed. Chase could see that, and he could tell how hard I was working and how important it was to me to build our relationship.

In a way, it also lessened the pressure on Chase. We were a great team, with me pushing Chase to near the breaking point and Ken taking Chase's side on any and every issue and always referencing anything I said back to "The Chosen One."

We were able to laugh at those comparisons, because the three of us were having the time of our lives working out together. The more Chase grew in strength and recognition in athletics, the more my good friend Ken stuck the needle in me. Along the way he even found the ultimate way to make sure Chase knew how proud I was of him.

Even though I thank Ken and I appreciate how he helped my relationship grow with my son, I think you will agree that one of his tactics was less than honorable.

Ken and I both are big people. I'm probably two inches taller than he is, and in my opinion, a whole lot better looking. People often question if we are brothers. I don't mind—I think he should feel proud. But my good friend used to do the most deplorable act that a man can do, especially to a friend.

Some people thought he, not I, was Chase's dad. Can you believe this guy didn't tell them any different? I mean, I don't blame him. Chase was already big and cut-up and strong. But to take credit for that—well, that is the ultimate low. It had me hustling around making sure everybody knew that I was Chase's daddy. Chasey loved that.

People in the gym, at school and at church were starting to take notice of how our relationship had grown. Cole Pittman was noticing, too.

When he came home from college and we all worked out together, he was out to prove that he, too, was someone to contend with in the weight room. If Chase grabbed a 100-pound dumbbell, Cole grabbed the 130-pound dumbbell.

By this time Cole had started a serious relationship with a girl he'd met at Texas. Later, Caren Lyons told me that when Cole was talking about how strong Chase was, he was quick to point out that if I had trained Cole in the gym, he would have been that strong in high school, too.

Caren said it was funny because you could tell he was jealous of the relationship.

And proud, too.

THIRTEEN

Learning to Love

WHILE WE CAN'T TRAVEL THE roads for our children, we certainly are responsible for making sure they take the right paths. We can't tell them which paths to take. That's against the rules. All we can do is explain to them the consequences of making the wrong choice.

Cole had made all the right decisions up to this point. He had traveled the right roads, but one obstacle was going to keep Cole from being successful. I could see it as plain as the nose on my face. I talked to him in quiet moments about it. That obstacle was Cole Pittman. He didn't like himself.

During Cole's nightly 9:30 phone calls, I encouraged him to live out his dreams. His passion for the University of Texas, for the game of football and for his teammates was all that he talked about.

In particular, Cole wanted to play defensive end, where he'd played most of his career, especially because one of the end positions was wide open. But he was slotted for defensive tackle, and he had to ask the coaches for a shot at end. Earning that starting defensive-end position was very important to Cole, and he worked extremely hard. But because he had to request the move, he thought the defensive end coach didn't really want him out there. Cole was going to prove him wrong.

All the hard work through the summer and spring paid off. Cole won the starting position as defensive end. He still felt like the defensive end coach had it in for him, a notion that didn't suffer when he lost that starting job to another player at midseason. Cole buttoned his lip, didn't say anything negative. But he was frustrated with the coach. He thought the man was not doing a very good job of showing him where the other kid was better.

Cole was one of those people who are extremely hard on themselves. He was also one of those people who, if he thought you expected something out of him and he liked you, he absolutely would not let you down. He would push himself to the total limit just trying to please you.

The coach just wanted to win ball games, and he wanted Cole to be better. His critical approach worked on some, but it had the opposite effect on Cole, who felt like the coach didn't like him. Cole lost about twenty pounds, and his productivity nose-dived.

Cole was frustrated, and he wasn't going to take it lying down. He even made the statement that when he graduated, he was going to go back and visit this coach. I agreed with him, "This will be the one coach that you will go back and thank. This will be that coach that pushed you to the next level."

Cole smiled. "You need to explain that to me, because I wasn't thinking about going to thank him," he said.

I looked him in the eyes. "Son, sometimes we travel life's road and we are on a trail we think we need to be on because it looks smooth and easy. Actually it's a dead-end road, and you end up banging your head on that dead end. You just need to find another way around to where you want to go. Life is going to be full of roads with obstacles, and you're going to have to learn when to fight and when to find another route."

Coach Brown had told me that he thought Cole had okay quickness for an end and great quickness for a tackle. The problem was convincing Cole that he needed to be playing inside instead of outside. I didn't have to. The defensive end coach did it for us.

For Cole to succeed at tackle he had to see himself as a tackle. Cole had a body structure with large bones; he could weigh 290 and be lean. At 247, it affected his strength. So I took him to a friend of mine who was a bodybuilder. This guy was only five-foot-nine, but he weighed 260 pounds.

I told Cole to take a good look at the bodybuilder.

"You can look like this at 290, 295 pounds," I said, "or look like skin and bones at 245, 250. That is your choice."

Cole not only made that transition in his mind, but he also made peace with that coach.

Cole had met a young woman named Caren Lyons, a petite blonde who played soccer at Texas. He had met her at a party and talked to her all night about everything, except for one important subject. He never asked for her phone number. The next day he beat the bushes good, calling every Lyons in the book, before he found her number.

His love for Caren was growing, and I knew I was going to have to share my time even when I went to Austin. He very seldom made the trip home without bringing her along. I knew this would happen. I also knew I couldn't fight it.

I give him this: When it came to personality, he couldn't have done any better. She laughed all the time. He had come to where he was talking about her family more and more. Like me, Caren's daddy was a contractor. Cole even went to some of the jobs with her father and looked them over. Cole didn't even need to tell me when he and Caren decided they would spend the rest of their lives together. All he did was change his major from kinesiology to construction.

Cole talked so highly about her family that I started thinking,

Man, I don't only have to compete with Caren; I have to compete with the whole family. Understand by now that I was a little afraid of meeting them.

When I finally met them, I knew why he liked them. Bob and Sue Lyons are wonderful people, firm but compassionate, strong but loving. Most importantly, I could see they were just as crazy about my son as he was about them.

Football season ended with the Holiday Bowl in San Diego, and Cole came home and spent a few days with us. We worked out, hunted and just spent time together: Cole, Chase and me. I was enjoying having both my boys with me. I wasn't anxious at all to let him go, but I knew he wasn't going to stay away from Caren very long.

School was going to start back in a couple of weeks, so he took a week's vacation with the Lyons family to Disney World in Orlando. He still called me every night at 9:30. When he returned, I was able to spend a couple more days with him. I told him that he looked like he hadn't missed a workout. He told me he hadn't, that he'd carried Riley, Caren's five-year-old nephew, on his shoulders the entire week.

School started, and Cole headed back to Austin with a renewed fire in his eyes. Not only did he realize that academics were important, but he had doubled up on his workout times. Even after the grueling workouts that were part of the normal off-season program, he would go back to the Moncrief-Neuhaus

Athletic Complex later and work out again with his good friend, Chance Mock.

—⁓—

When I talk about being a success in life, I'm not talking about having money. I'm talking about building relationships and how many people you can touch in a positive way while here on earth. Remember, I had traveled this same road, and it had taken forty years to find myself, a journey I couldn't have made if my kids hadn't helped show me the way. I didn't want Cole to wait until he was forty to begin to like who he was. I thought if I could convince him of just how much he had to offer, then it would alter his opinion of himself.

With that in mind, I began to encourage him to speak in public. I promised him that if he would speak on three different occasions, then I would never ask him to speak again. To me, he had an obvious ability to communicate with people. Once he began to relate with these people through talks, I felt he would realize that he had something to offer, and that would help him over this barrier.

Being a football player at the University of Texas meant people wanted to hear what he said. Cole was adamant that he wasn't a speaker and that he didn't have anything to say that anybody would want to hear.

If God wants you to do something, there is no getting out of it. That was the message I wanted to put across to my son, and I reminded him of the story of Jonah being swallowed up by a whale.

Cole and a couple other football players were invited to a fundraiser for abused children. Cole loved kids. He thought he was going to go and interact with these kids. That was easy for him. When he arrived, though, he found out there was only one kid at the whole affair, and he happened to be the son of a high school coach.

Nobody told Cole he was going to speak. He hadn't prepared anything, but he knew he couldn't say no. Scared to death, he just walked up there and started talking.

That night Cole called me at eleven o'clock. He was absolutely ecstatic. He thought he would be nervous, but he was relaxed. He was so excited after speaking to these people. He was ready to do it again and again, but he'd never get the chance.

Looking back, I can honestly say I don't know if I'd ever seen Cole this happy. I could hear it in his voice, and I could tell it from his phone calls. Sometimes he'd call me as many as four or five times a day just to tell me how much he loved me. The calls came so often they made me feel like I was getting behind. He didn't even give me time to call him and tell him how much I loved him.

Now even though a Love War may be the only war in

someone's life they would want to lose, you still have to fight back. Cole's birthday was coming up, so I thought I would take a shot at him. On January 25, the eve of his twenty-first birthday, I drove five hours one way just to have dinner with him and Caren. After dinner we dropped Caren off at her apartment and then we rode around and talked for about an hour before it was time for me to be heading back to Shreveport. He asked me to stay the night. I knew better. I explained to him that I knew that on your birthday, especially your twenty-first birthday, you didn't want to spend it sitting around some dorm room with Dad. I told him he needed to spend his evening with Caren, and I would be fine. I had things I needed to do at home.

At two-thirty in the morning I was flying down Highway 79, just short of Palestine, when my cell phone rang. It was Cole.

"Dad, I love you so much."

And then the question.

"Dad, how many dads in this world would drive ten hours just to have dinner with their son on his twenty-first birthday?" Cole asked.

I had been teaching Cole and Chase that you don't just tell somebody you love them; you have to show them. Cole's statement that night as I traveled through Palestine made me appreciate the fact that he had been listening.

Since my boy died I've often told other people, "Don't worry about how much your kids love you. Worry about how much you love your kids. And show them." Then I'd make the same state-ment to the kids. "Don't worry about how much your parents love you, but how much you love your parents. And show them."

Nothing comes without cost. This cost me some sleep and a lot of driving miles, but I was so glad I did it.

FOURTEEN

If You Had Two
Final Days…

THE DAY IS FEBRUARY 24, 2001. If you were going to spend two final days with someone you loved, how would you spend them?

———

The first week of January 2001, I was sitting in the First Assembly of God church in Shreveport listening to Pastor Denny Duron preach about the Prayer of Jabez. It was so simple, yet so direct, it captured my soul. I began to get up every morning at five o'clock, hit my knees and recite the Prayer of Jabez from 1 Chronicles 4:10 over my son.

"Oh God, bless Cole indeed and enlarge his territory, that your hand would be upon him, and that you would keep him from evil, that he would cause no harm!"

At first it gnawed at me. When I said the prayer each morning, was I saying it as a selfish prayer? Was that what I was doing?

I thought about it one morning while doing my daily Bible reading and couldn't find my reading glasses. I knew there was a pair in Judy's office in the house, so I went there to get them, all the while chewing it over. *Would my son be glorified? Or would God be glorified?* I wanted an answer.

As I passed the laundry area I saw a book sitting on the dryer. Believe it or not, it was *The Prayer of Jabez* by Bruce H. Wilkinson, the best-selling author. When I finished reading it, I understood I wasn't being selfish. I was asking God to bless my son.

On February 24, a typical Saturday morning at our lakefront town home, I rose at 4 A.M. to say the Prayer of Jabez and read the Bible. Then I headed to the driveway to pick up the morning newspaper. Much to my surprise and joy there sat a red Chevy truck in the driveway, with Cole asleep behind the wheel. He had driven all night from Austin, getting in at two-thirty in the morning. Knowing that if he came in he would wake me up and I wouldn't go back to sleep, he roughed it in the truck.

I was so excited to see him, I dragged him out of the truck, covered him with kisses and dragged him into the house to Mama. After Judy added her kisses on top of mine, we put him in our bed, told him to catch some sleep and we would talk when he woke up. When he did, we just sat around and talked most of the day. Cole decided to go to a Mardi Gras party in town with a few of his friends.

There was something different about Cole this weekend. I mean, he was so radiant that he glowed. I had never seen him this happy, and I hadn't seen him this big. He was huge. His trapezius muscles seemed to start almost beneath his ears and ran out over his shoulders, swallowing any evidence of a neck. His chest was much larger than I had ever seen it, but he was still pretty cut. I had never seen his arms this big. You could see the confidence in the way he walked. But most important of all, I could tell Cole was starting to like who he was.

On most nights when our boys went out, Judy or I waited up until they came in. Chase's curfew was midnight, but with Cole being there and us trusting him so much, we went on to bed.

Sunday morning we went to church. Cole stood beside me, wearing one of my shirts and a pair of Chase's pants because he had not brought any church clothes. My best friend Ken Meeks came up behind us and told my boy, "Well, Cole, you've always wanted to be bigger than your daddy. You have arrived. You make your daddy look like a pencil-neck basketball player."

I pretended I was hurt, but I was swelling with pride. Both boys lived for the day that they would be bigger than me. The two things you would never see me become truly upset about were that one day my boys would grow bigger than me and that they would ultimately win the Love Wars.

Cole had brought his radiant joy to church with him. Several people picked up on it. Coach Dennis Dunn's wife, Melanie, went home after church and called her husband, who was out of town.

"You should have seen Cole today. He looks unbelievable," she remembered telling him.

The plan was for us to have lunch together, hug and kiss and love each other, then send Cole on his way back to Austin by three o'clock that afternoon. Spring football was scheduled to start that Monday morning with a ten o'clock meeting, and Cole wanted to make a great impression on his first day as a full-time defensive tackle.

I was surprised when he came and asked me, "Dad, would you mind too much if I spent the rest of the afternoon with you and just leave when you get up in the morning? I'll have plenty of time."

Frankly, I was glad to have him stay. I certainly wasn't looking forward to him going back, then or later. He and I went out and got in the Jeep Wrangler, took the top off and just starting riding around, holding hands and talking. We rode around and looked at some properties that I thought might be good investments. I told him my dreams, and he told me his. To me this was one of the best afternoons that I had ever spent with Cole, just visiting, laughing and talking.

We came upon a lady who had a flat at the intersection of Ockley and Line. She was struggling to pull the jack out of her vehicle. We pulled over and in just a few minutes we had that tire changed.

She was so grateful for the help.

"Son, what do I owe you?" she asked Cole.

Cole grinned his best aw-shucks grin.

"Ma'am, if you will just smile for me and promise me that you will have a good day," he said, "then we've been paid enough."

Soon the sun started creeping below the horizon, and it was starting to get a little cool to be riding around in that Jeep. I asked Cole if he was ready to head back to the house.

"Let's make one more stop," he said.

Cole wanted to see Coach Ronnie Alexander, his old defensive coordinator at Evangel. As they sat and talked football, I couldn't help but notice how close they'd become. Cole made it a point to let Coach A know he wasn't going to let his football coaching go to waste. Cole was going back to Austin to fulfill his dreams.

After we ate dinner at home, Cole sat next to me on the couch. We watched a movie together. Chase had been over at his girlfriend's house and walked in about the time the movie was ending. I cautioned Cole about staying up too late, because he would have to get up early. I didn't know until later that after watching the movie with me, he and Chase rented a movie they hadn't seen since they were kids. They went up into Chase's room and lay there and watched that movie together.

When I think back on all he did that day and the grace and joy with which he did it, how he glowed so bright, I wonder if he knew that this day would be his last day on earth.

If you had only two final days, how would you spend them?

———∿∿∿———

It was still dark when I went into his room at four-thirty and shook him awake. Judy fixed him some peanut butter sand-wiches, a bottle of water and a large cup of coffee for his trip. Three times he walked out the front door to head to his truck. Three times he came back in and kissed his mother good-bye.

When we finally made it out the door I walked him to the truck, arm-in-arm. As we stood before the truck I once again prayed the Jabez prayer over him: "Oh God, bless Cole indeed and enlarge his territory, that your hand would be upon him, and that you would keep him from evil, that he would cause no harm!"

When I finished I kissed him.

"Son, you go back to Austin," I told him. "You bless God, and He will bless you."

"Dad," Cole said, "I love you so much."

Cole climbed in the cab and started the ignition. He looked at me and smiled. Then he backed up down the driveway, popped it in drive and headed toward the front gate of the community.

Normally when I saw my son off to school, after the truck went out of sight I'd turn and walk back into the house. That morning, for reasons I couldn't then understand, I walked out to the brick mailbox at the end of the drive and stood rooted. I just stood there and listened to the loud pipes on his truck as he roared down Willowridge Boulevard to Lakeshore Drive and out to Loop 220, which would start taking him back to Austin. The roar seemed to go on forever and ever and ever. When the sound finally faded, I turned and walked back to the house. Looking up, I noticed Judy standing at the door, tears in her eyes. She had been listening too.

FIFTEEN

Left Behind

IT'S FUNNY. YOU SUFFER THROUGH something like losing a son, and sometimes it's the little things you think about.

Cole didn't have his cell phone with him that day.

I think about what difference that could have made. Usually I called him three or four times on his trip back. Usually he called me three or four times.

If he'd had that phone, maybe one of those calls would have come as he sped down a lonely mile of road on Highway 79, just a few miles east of Franklin, Texas.

Even today I'll pick up my cell phone, punch forty-four—his uniform number—on the speed dial and hit send.

It was approaching ten o'clock Monday morning. I knew he

would be arriving there close to the time of the meeting, but I had told him to try and give me a call when he made it to Austin so I would know he was okay.

Ten o'clock came and went. I thought maybe he had arrived just in time to go to his meeting and didn't have time to call. I went through the normal day, thinking about him, worrying about him, but feeling like he was okay. He'd call.

About one-thirty, I grew anxious. I called Caren's apartment and left her a message to tell Cole to be sure and call so I would know he was okay. At two o'clock, knowing I should have heard from him by now, I called back and left another message. I was starting to get a knot in the pit of my stomach.

A few minutes later, Wanda Allen, my business partner, walked in and said one of my sisters had called to tell me to stay in the office, that she was coming to see me. I knew immediately that something had happened to someone in my family. I still did not want to believe that it was one of my children.

I called Caren again. Still no answer. I left a frantic message to please have Cole call, that something had happened to somebody in the family and I was worried about him. I didn't know what had happened, but please call.

My cell phone rang; it was Ronnie Alexander, my friend and Cole's favorite coach. I told him I couldn't talk, that something had happened to somebody in my family and I was trying to find out who it was. I hung up.

What I didn't realize was that he was on his way to the office, too. He and the entire Evangel coaching staff. When I heard them come in the front door of the office, my blood went cold.

Ronnie was the first one in my office. His legs buckled and he fell to his knees in front of me, weeping. He kept telling me how sorry he was.

"Was it Chase? Something wrong with Chase?" I asked, thinking that because they were in town and had been around Chase, something had happened to him. They just looked at me.

"Is it Cole?" I asked.

They began to weep.

"Is he dead?" I screamed. They couldn't even tell me.

I picked up the phone and called Judy. I said, "Come to the office now." Then I dialed the University of Texas. Mack Brown answered the phone. He was weeping uncontrollably.

"Tell me my boy is there next to you," I said, hoping against hope. "They're trying to tell me he's dead. Tell me he's standing there next to you."

"I wish I could," Mack said, and he began crying. "Marc, what do you want me to tell the kids?" he said.

I thought about what Cole would want me to tell the kids.

"Coach," I said as steadily as I could, "just tell them I love them."

I hung up the phone.

I didn't know what to feel. I was not crying. I was numb. I was mad. I stood up and looked at the coaches, and I began to quote the Jabez prayer, each word steeped in sarcasm. I looked at the heavens as I fairly spat out the words: Enlarge his territory, that your hand would be upon him, that you would keep him from evil. . . . OH, YOU BLESSED HIM ALL RIGHT. . . .

Was this God's idea of enlarging Cole's territory? What kind of God would do that to this boy? Why would God do this to me? I had been doing what I was supposed to be doing. Cole had been doing what he was supposed to be doing. Why did God let us down? Cole Pittman may not have been a perfect person, but Cole Pittman was the perfect son. For the first time in my life I was facing something that I just didn't know how to handle. I just wanted to be alone. I walked out of the office and toward the warehouse, trying to get myself together.

As I wandered in circles, a sudden, strange peace began coming over me. I began to understand. God didn't take Cole. God needed Cole more than I did, more than this world did. At that moment God and I came to an agreement. God told me that if I honor him, he will honor this boy. He'll bless him. He'll enlarge his territory.

A police car sat in the driveway. Then I saw Judy turn into the driveway and step out of her car. The coaches and the policeman had followed me outside, keeping their distance, and they saw Judy drive up. When she climbed out of the car, I was perhaps forty yards away. She took one look at me and started backing up. She started screaming.

"No, I don't want to hear this. Get away from me." Judy started running down the street, screaming. She ran into the middle of the vacant lot and collapsed. The coaches ran to her side to comfort her. I was still mad as hell. I walked up to her and screamed.

"It's Cole. He's gone."

I turned and walked back to my truck and went looking for Chase.

By now it was a little after three. Chase would be coming to the house, so that's where I headed. On the way I called Ken Meeks at The Plex. He wasn't there. I left a message for him, telling him that I wouldn't be there to work out today, that Cole had been killed in an auto accident.

When I made it to the house, Chase wasn't there yet. I started back to the vehicle to look for him when he drove up. From the look on my face, he knew something was wrong.

"What's wrong?" he said softly.

My anger hadn't totally passed. I was brutal. I just looked at him and said, "Your brother has been killed in an automobile accident."

Chase just turned and starting running toward the back of the house. I hated myself for the way I told him. I went through the house to cut him off, to tackle him, to hold him. I found him in the corner of the house, curled up in a little ball, weeping hysterically. I tried to console him, but I didn't have any words worth saying.

That afternoon I learned what happened to my boy. Sometime just after 7:30, about 110 miles from Austin, he missed a turn on Highway 79, hit a guardrail and went airborne. His truck nose-dived into the far bank of a creek and flipped over. The feeling was that he had been killed instantly. The justice of the peace pronounced him dead at 8:15 that morning. I'll always remember that time.

I later learned that a former Longhorn letterman named Thomas "Bubba" Phillips happened on the scene about a half hour later and spoke to the tow-truck driver, who said he saw a ring from Texas's 1999 Big 12 championship game with the name Pittman on it. Phillips called Texas, but they hadn't yet heard any word.

By early evening people began to gather at the house. I still wasn't showing any emotion, though the tension was so tight I thought my head would explode. Coach Johnny Booty at Evangel had taken care of having Cole's body brought back to Shreveport. It's hard to remember much of what transpired that afternoon. I do remember one thing, and that was me asking someone, "Do you think it's because I'm no good?"

A front had moved in. It had begun to rain: a cold, light shower. About ten o'clock I walked out on the back deck and stared out into the darkness over Cross Lake. Then I looked up at the sky. Cold rain hit me in the face. I closed my eyes. I wanted God to tell me this wasn't so. I wanted God to tell me that it was just a bad dream.

Every time it rains now, I relive that moment. I go outside and let the drops hit me in the face.

Our pastor, Denny Duron, had just flown back into town and came straight to the house. He put his arm around me and started crying and shaking. For the first time my emotions cracked. I was about to experience the longest night of my life. I knew the next day I would be seeing my son, but he wouldn't be able to talk to me. I knew that when he had driven off that morning, I had heard it for the last time. "Dad, I love you so much."

Ken Meeks and Ronnie Alexander hadn't left my side all day. They sat with me all night, taking turns catnapping on the couch.

When the sun finally came up I got up. There were things we needed to do. We needed to go to a men's store to get a bigger coat for Cole to be buried in because, with all his hard work in the weight room, none of his coats would fit. I wore a fifty-six long. Cole was going to need a fifty-eight. There was a time that fact would have made me so proud. Now I felt nothing.

As we drove to Davis' Men's Store with Ken and Ronnie in the back, I turned and asked Judy, "Do you think I marked Cole for death by naming him after Jerry Brandon, because he was killed in a car accident?"

Ronnie Alexander looked startled. "Do you mean Jerry Brandon, the Blond Bomber? Who went to Louisiana Tech?" he asked. "Do you mean Cole was named after him?"

I nodded.

"He was my best friend," Ronnie said.

In my mind I guess I was still trying to figure out why Cole Pittman had to die. We left there and went to the funeral home to pick out his casket. They had a big selection, but they only had two that would accommodate his shoulder width. One of them was the one I would have picked out if there had been a thousand of them. It was blue steel, simple and sturdy, rugged and tough, just like Cole. While we were there they gave us the personal effects they'd recovered from Cole's truck. I took the Big 12 championship game ring and slipped it on my right hand.

My family was helping plan the funeral. My sister asked me if I would like for someone in the family to speak and even volunteered her husband. I thanked her but said no. I didn't feel like I wanted anybody to say anything. It didn't seem like anybody could say anything that would be enough.

There was one more thing to do, the hardest thing of all. I would have to go back to the funeral home and see my lifeless son for the first time.

I was more scared than I have ever been in my life. I didn't know if I would be able to handle it. But I had Judy under one arm and Chase under the other. What choice did I have?

I can remember my knees started to buckle as we approached the door. I didn't know if I could continue. Then an amazing thing happened. When I saw Cole lying there, an unreal surge of energy went through me. I think God just showed up. I knew what I had to do. I turned and looked at Denny Duron, and I said, "I'll speak at my son's funeral."

Denny was a rock for me. I told him that as I looked back over my life, every time there was a low, it seemed I only went higher as a result of it. I wondered if that could possibly still be true, and if so, just how high would I go now? "Life is a big puzzle," I often told my boys. Each piece has to fit in order for you to make it to where you are today. I told them I didn't regret anything that had ever happened in my life, because it made me the person that I am, and I liked who I am. But this piece? I've got to tell you I was struggling mightily with it.

They moved Cole to the church for his viewing. The rain hadn't let up. People began to line up to pass by his coffin. I stood there by Cole, and when the first ones came through I started hugging them. It didn't stop. I had never experienced or seen anything like this in my life. People were sharing our pain. They estimated around four thousand people came that night. Women, children, adults. Men I had never seen before. For three-and-a-half hours I hugged. I hugged every one of them.

Someone told Denny that he should stop the people from hugging me, that I would not be able to hold up. But Denny could see what they couldn't, that I was getting my energy from them. They blessed me with their testimonies. I'll never forget one young man about Cole's age. He told me he'd met Cole at that Mardi Gras party he went to the Saturday before he died.

The man told me he'd been drinking heavily. When he decided to head home, Cole wouldn't let him drive. Cole drove him home, witnessing to him all the way.

My son had one more night in this world, and Denny knew I'd want to spend it with him. He gave me a key to the church. I went and got a blanket and a pillow. Ken volunteered to stay with me, but I told him I wanted to be alone. He understood, and told me he would stay at the back of the church if I needed him.

I snuggled up as close to the coffin as I could get. I'd brought a pen and pad, knowing that in a few short hours I'd be talking over my son, trying to honor him the way he had honored me for twenty-one years.

At dawn I left the church. I went home, splashed some water on my face, ran a comb through my hair and changed my clothes. I took a long look in the mirror. Then I headed back to my boy.

Rain continued to fall, like it would never stop. People began to arrive. They just kept coming and coming, until the sanctuary at the First Assembly of God was packed with between three and four thousand people. The last ones to enter were the University of Texas football coaches and staff, and then the players, six of whom carried Cole to his grave.

I told Denny I could speak only if he didn't play any music beforehand. I knew that if I heard a song, any song, I would become too emotional. I didn't want to be emotional. I'd been to too many funerals and seen too many loved ones try to talk through their tears, and be impossible to understand. I didn't want that to happen with Cole. I thought maybe if I just didn't look at him and they didn't play the music, then I might be able to hold it together.

As I hugged the Texas coaches, the choir struck its first note. They were singing "How Great Thou Art," a song that was sung at my father's funeral. For years after his death I fell to my knees when I heard the first notes of the song. But a strange thing happened that day. I felt that same surge of energy as when I first saw my boy in his coffin. God showed up, and it was all I could do to keep from praising him. I had never felt so strong in all of my life.

When the choir fell silent, Denny approached the podium and announced that I would be speaking. There wasn't any fear in me anymore. I walked over to the casket, leaned over, kissed my son and asked him, "Son, tell me what you want me to say. Tell me what you want me to tell the people."

As I approached the podium, I could feel the presence of God so heavily in this place. It was unbelievable. As I picked up the microphone, I was amazed at the strength in my voice.

PART TWO

*F*irst, I want to thank everybody for being here. It's a tribute to what Cole did in life. It blesses me. A lot of you have said, "I don't know what to say," or "I can't say anything to help." You are wrong. It helps and it's meant the world to me. It has lifted me up.

A special thanks to Ken Meeks and Ronnie Alexander, they have been literally underneath my arms since I heard about this. Without them it would have been a tougher deal. Also Dennis Dunn and Evangel Christian Academy. They and the church family, they have been a blessing. And the University of Texas and Coach Mack Brown. I love you guys, I love you all. Thank you, thank you for coming!

But most of all, my son, Chasey, you've got to hold me up. I could not be here at all if it wasn't for you. I could not be here without you to hold me up. I'm wallowing in deep water, and it's cold and my soul hurts. Don't turn my hand loose! Okay?

When Cole was about ten years old, I went to pick him up at a Royal Ambassadors meeting. He had been in a fight at a church and the lady was livid, and she jumped all over me and I jumped all over Cole and I reamed him out pretty good. I asked him what was the fight about? And he said, "There were two big guys picking on a little guy, and I didn't think it was fair, so I whipped both of them!"

It was hard to be mad at him after that, but you know it when you open a door of opportunity. That door of opportunity was to sit down and talk with him, and we often did. I said, "Son, you were fighting in church. The reason was commendable, but you were fighting in church, and that lady doesn't know the reason. And so you have hurt my name. I loved my daddy, and my daddy's name is all I have. Son, that's my name and don't you ever hurt my name."

When Cole got ready to go to the University of Texas, we traveled the road to Texas. I pondered about what I would tell Cole. When he said good-bye to his mother and Chase, we sent them out of the room, and then I hugged him and I said to him, "Son, your name is Pittman. Now what are you going to do with it?"

Well, he made national news, made people fly hundreds of miles to see him. He was literally all over the Internet. He was in USA Today. As I understood Mack Brown last night, even the president of the United States had called and sent his condolences. What more could he do! Praise God!

He did what he said he would do.

You might wonder why I can stand up here and speak over Cole. Well, I have two sons. Both of them have honored me and honored God. I will not dishonor my son by not saying something on his behalf.

When he drove off Monday morning, we left absolutely nothing unsaid. There is nothing I could call Cole Pittman back and tell him that I have not already told him. We lived every day just like it was our last. You don't understand just how close me and this boy are. This boy has been at college two years, a few days, and every night at 9:30 you could put your hand on the phone and Cole Pittman was going to call his daddy, just to say, "I love you." Sometimes he would call me five or six times a day just to say, "What's up!" and I would say, "What's up with you, big boy?" And Cole would say, "Dad, I love you so much!"

If y'all were to ask me who I would most like to be in this world, I would have to tell you I would like to be like my two sons, not because they've got parents that have spoiled them, but because they have taught me so much. They have taught me so much that I am perplexed how they can love me the way they love me. I am continuously trying to show them ways that I love them just as much.

If Cole was here, and I will speak for him, this is what he would say to you: Kiss your children every day. Talk to your children every day. Do you tell them that you love them every day? Do you show them that you love them every day?

A good friend of mine, Jack Rothell, told me yesterday that he learned it's okay to openly express your love for your children. What I found out is that when you openly love your children like that, other kids come around because they want that same feel-good feeling. And that, my friends, is why Evangel Academy kids and University of Texas kids come up and hug me. They see me hug my kids, and they come up to get that same feeling.

God said about Jesus, "This is my son, and I am well pleased." There is no way I'll compare Cole to Jesus, but this is what I will say: "This is my son, I am well pleased!"

There is nothing I can say about Cole that's worthy enough to honor him, but what I am going to ask you to do is to honor his memory by making God and family your priority…

A lot of people seem to think I was Cole's best friend. Cole's best friend was his brother, Chase. And what more could a daddy ask for than to be blessed with his two sons being best friends!

And once again, My Son, My Son, My Son, I ask you, Son, to hold me up. Daddy is trying hard!

I love you so much!

SIXTEEN

"How Many Saturdays?"

WE MADE THE FORTY-FIVE-MINUTE drive from First Assembly to Fellowship Cemetery in a steady rain. When we arrived there, the rain let up. I'll always remember that, just as I'll always remember every detail about the ceremony. The gray, overcast sky. The smell of freshly turned dirt. The agony and the emptiness. Deanza Duron singing "Amazing Grace." The University of Texas football team gathering at the foot of Cole's grave, holding their hands up in the Hook 'em Horns sign and softly singing "The Eyes of Texas."

I can't remember how many times Denny Duron had preached on the theme of asking us how many Saturdays each of us has left. He asked the question only to remind us that none are promised. It didn't matter if you came from a line of healthy stock or if your ancestors lived long lives. None of that mattered. Every day you had to live as if next Saturday might be your last—if you even made it to Saturday.

In his eulogy Denny revised the theme. "If we just count Saturdays," he said, "it won't be long until we're all together."

Denny also spoke of Cole being alive and with us in another dimension. Maybe it was that suggestion, but I noticed a flock of geese flying overhead in a loose formation that looked to form a letter "C." And they were quiet. Geese are never quiet when they're flying.

The next day we were to go to Austin for a memorial service at the University of Texas Performing Arts Center, but we were just exhausted. I knew I wouldn't be able to make the five-hour drive, not after another sleepless night. But Red McCombs, owner of the Minnesota Vikings and a Texas Exe, sent his private plane for us. Later I tried to write a letter to him, thanking him for his kindness, but I couldn't adequately find the words to express what he'd meant to us. I'd never met him. When I did later, it wasn't his financial standing that impressed me most. It was the size of his heart.

Ronnie Alexander and Ken Meeks weren't about to leave me alone, so they made the flight with me, Judy, Chase and his girl-friend, Britni. Our friends, Jimmy and Kathy Rawls, drove to Austin so they could bring Cole's possessions back with them.

The Evangel coaching staff came over as a group.

They took us to the Moncrief-Neuhaus Complex to meet with the team. When I walked in, a player hugged me and then hugged Judy and then hugged Chase. Each player stood up and hugged us. The line wasn't getting any shorter. After they hugged us, some players went back in line to do it again.

Then it was time to begin the walk to the memorial service. As we came out of the tunnel that the team used to enter the field at Royal-Memorial Stadium, I looked at strength coach Jeff "Mad Dog" Madden. "Let's do it for Cole," I said.

Madden understood. He gathered the team around him, as they usually did before games. They started bouncing up and down and chanting. I just had to hear it one more time.

We began to walk across the field. The rain had stopped. Above the tunnel, high on the JumboTron scoreboard, was a picture of Cole, my big, beautiful son, looking down on us. At midfield the players stopped, turned toward Cole's picture and sang "The Eyes of Texas." Oh, how he'd loved Texas.

Texas never does anything halfway. They went all out. All the athletic teams were there. So were hundreds of fans, some of whom had never met Cole. A guitar player sang Willie Nelson's "The Healing Hands of Time," a song Nelson had written about the death of one of his own children. Mack Brown spoke. Two of Cole's teammates, Ahmad Brooks and Matt Trissel, shared their memories of Cole. And I did my part to honor my son.

Then came the hardest part. We went to Cole's dorm room, where I had hugged him good-bye on his twenty-first birthday just a month earlier, and packed up his belongings.

Our plane took off for Shreveport that evening in the midst of a thunderstorm. Lighting flashed outside the windows, and the plane shook. I looked over to see Judy silently praying. Ronnie Alexander had his jaw set. Ken Meeks white-knuckled the arm supports. I didn't care. If the plane went down, I'd have laughed all the way to the ground. We would all be together again.

The next morning, Judy and I loaded up a bunch of the potted plants that had been given as a tribute to Cole. We were going to share them with my family in Dubberly as we made our return trip to the cemetery. By now the numbness was wearing off and the pain was settling in. I would never wish this on my worst enemies. The agony of losing your child is enough, but it wasn't just my pain. It was hearing Judy lay there at night and that soft, mournful wailing as she cried over missing her baby. It was knowing Chase was hurting but not being able to do anything about it.

We were determined that we were going to hold each other up, but I needed more than that. I needed compassion from my family. I needed their help. I didn't get it. When we arrived at my mother's house, where everyone was congregating, I hadn't walked in the door before I was set upon.

I know my family has come to love me, but they were already giving advice. One by one they said some variation of "Chase is not Cole. Don't you dare expect Chase to follow in Cole's shoes." Not once did anyone say one word that I could find comforting. We didn't hang around long. As we walked to the truck, Judy started weeping and she said, "Why can't they just mourn with us? Why can't they allow us to grieve? Why do they feel they need to attack you?"

I didn't have any answers for that.

At the cemetery we wept over our boy's grave. We talked to him, pouring out our feelings. Then Judy made a request. "Son, we are struggling, and we need to know you're okay. We need to know you are with us. We need a sign. Would you give us some forty-fours when we struggle? Would you give us some forty-fours to let us know you're with us?"

Forty-fours starting popping up everywhere. I get chills as I sit here and write about it. The mile marker was forty-four. The exit number was forty-four. License plate after license plate had a forty-four. That was just the beginning.

I was worried about Chase. I still felt awful about how I'd broken the news to him about his brother's death, and I felt inadequate that I couldn't find the words to comfort him. I thought that was odd because I had recently comforted several people who had lost loved ones. Just two week before Cole's death I was watching *The O'Reilly Factor* as host Bill O'Reilly interviewed a lady who had written a book about dealing with the death of a loved one. Judy shook her head. "You could have written that book," she said. "She's said everything that you have always said." I can tell you this, though. It's one thing when it's someone else's child or someone else's loved one; it's different when it's your own.

Later that morning, I received a call from the school. Chase was struggling. That day and for days afterward, I went every morning and spent some time with Chase at school during first period, trying to help him through this. He was having a hard time showing emotion, and people were giving him advice.

"Dad, people are telling me I just need to let it loose," Chase told me. "That I need to do this or I need to do that."

I kissed his face.

"Son, can you tell me of a better relationship than I had with Cole or that I have with you?"

"No, sir."

"Son, can you tell me of two brothers who were closer than you and Cole? Two brothers who are both six-foot-four and who still kiss and hug each other? Still call each other every day and tell each other that they love them? Can you name one relationship that is better than that?"

"No, sir."

"Then who can tell you or me how we are supposed to feel? However we feel, that's the way we are supposed to feel. No one, Son, can tell us how we are supposed to feel or how we are supposed to act."

As tough as this first week was for me, in some ways it was tougher for Judy. A friend of hers, seeing the emphasis placed on mine and Cole's relationship, was probably trying to make Judy feel better when she asked her, "Didn't Cole have a mother?"

It had the opposite effect. After Judy hung up the phone in the kitchen, she walked into the den and fell on her knees, weeping. "Tell me I was a good mother," she sobbed. "Please tell me I was a good mother." Then she told me what the friend had said.

First I was angry with the friend, even though I suspected she meant well. But I've always been an advocate of trying to find something good in something bad, and this may have been one of the best things that happened. It opened up an opportunity for me to tell Judy just how good a mother she was. Granted, my boys and I did have a strong relationship, but how many mamas would sit back and do the hard part? She did the cooking, the cleaning and the nursing, did her share of paddling the boys with wooden spoons, and never—not one time—did she ever begrudge my relationships with Cole and Chase. Not one time did she interfere in the Dead Man's Talks. I don't know if there is another woman in the world who would have done what she did. I honestly believe she is the best mother in the world, and I told her so.

We were pulling our world back together as best we could. But there was one more thing I needed to do for my boy.

SEVENTEEN

Tributes

I HAD HONORED MY SON BY keeping his memory alive at his funeral and memorial service. I had tried to pull my other son closer, to pull my wife closer. I tried to do what I could to ease their pain.

Now I would go see where my son died.

It had been almost two weeks since Cole died and five days since I gave my cabinetmaker a special order.

He was to build a cross, a huge, red oak cross made out of an eight-by-eight timber, ripped down to a four-by-four, with beveled edges and ends. It would be six feet high and four feet wide.

When I saw it, it was absolutely beautiful. I wrapped the bottom eighteen inches, the part I'd cement into the ground, in copper so it wouldn't deteriorate. I told my foreman to put a sealer on it. No stain, just a natural sealer. I wanted natural wood. So he put a couple of coats of sealer on it, sanded it and put the third coat on.

When I saw it that Friday morning I thought it was perfect. The finish was like glass. I told him just how pretty I thought it was, but he told me he wasn't satisfied with it and wanted to work on it some more. He loved Cole, and he wanted to do something special for him. I told him that would be fine, that I was leaving in the morning to erect it at the crash site. It would have to be ready.

The foreman took some steel wool, buffed down the cross and put another coat of sealer on it. Because he was afraid it wouldn't dry, he took a kerosene heater with a blower on it and angled it toward the cross so he would be sure it was ready for me to take the next morning.

Friday night at ten o'clock I went up to get it, to affix a brass plate I'd had inscribed with the words I'd uttered at his birth—"My Son, My Son, My Son"—and a simple inscription that read, "In life you touched the world. In death you rocked it." I also had a Longhorn head on the plaque with the number forty-four on each side of it.

When I saw the cross I was stunned. The heat had turned it as burnt orange as a Texas jersey. It was absolutely beautiful. I get chills when I talk about it.

Next morning, about three o'clock, I left for Franklin. Judy had picked up the compact disc of Willie Nelson's "The Healing Hands of Time." For the next three-and-a-half hours I played that song over and over and over again. I wailed, I cried, I moaned, and I just plain hurt. The only time that I didn't have the song on was when I recorded two letters: One to Mack Brown for all that he had done and one to former Texas coach Darrell Royal, who had touched my heart so much and who had lost two children of his own to auto accidents.

By the time I approached the wreck site and eased my truck off the edge of the road onto the grassy shoulder, my shirt was wet from having cried so much. I walked back and looked at the deep ravine. Scattered around were small pieces of his truck. I just wanted to die. I paced about a quarter-mile up and down the road, tracing the impression his tire tracks left as the truck left the road.

I took the cross out of the back of the truck, dug a nice, deep hole with the post hole digger and set the cross. I walked back. I looked at it. I pulled it up and I moved it. I walked back to look again. When I finally had it where I wanted it, I set it in concrete.

The day before, I had called the Texas Department of Public Safety trooper who had worked the accident to tell him I'd be coming by. He informed me that he had all of Cole's possessions and that it would be better if I didn't go see the truck, just to come by his house. When I had the cross where it needed to be and everything in place, I hung a wreath on it and headed to the trooper's house.

He could see my pain. He was very polite. I followed him to the courthouse where he had stored Cole's belongings. As we had loaded everything up, he turned and looked at me and said, "Mr. Pittman, we found some muscle relaxers in Cole's bag. You think he may have taken some muscle relaxers that caused him to fall asleep?"

I told him I didn't think Cole would have done that, but he had been working out twice a day and his back was hurting very much. Driving was harder on it than anything else so, yeah, maybe he had done that.

I headed back home, playing "The Healing Hands of Time" and crying all the way. When I arrived at the house, Judy came out, buried her face in his clothes and began to sob hysterically. We began to go through his stuff and gently put it in places so we could save it for another time.

We had grown very close to Caren, trying to be each other's source of strength. She was back in Houston with her parents, so we called each other three and four times a day.

One night as we were talking she said, "Mr. Pittman, I dreamed about Cole. He looked wonderful." She described what he had on, his favorite shirt. She said they walked around the

Texas campus all day long, holding hands and talking. She asked him, "Cole, a lot of people are upset. What happened?" Cole told her, "I stopped in Palestine and got something to drink, took a couple of muscle relaxers and I fell asleep."

Odd thing was, I hadn't told Caren about the muscle relaxers. And when we had gone through his wallet, we found the receipt that showed he had bought a soft drink in Palestine.

—❧—

I was still searching for ways to channel my grief, when Ronnie Alexander and I found a project that was perfect. There was a classified advertisement for an old houseboat, a real junker, a fifteen-by-fifty-foot rust bucket. I bought it for four thousand dollars.

The problem was getting it to my shop. It was late on a Friday. I asked Allen Davidson, a deputy sheriff who escorted the buses to the Evangel games, for a favor. He knew Cole well, even had Cole ride with him on most of the trips. He told us he'd give us an escort in the morning.

That next day, we hauled that houseboat to the shop and I started a restoration project second to none. I did everything to that boat. I installed a complete kitchen, two gas grills, a fishing boat and a sun deck. I painted it burnt orange and white. We named it *Cole's Place,* putting a big sign on the front with a six-foot-five-inch pair of Longhorns between the words. I even found some burnt orange furniture to put in it.

About two months later, about eight o'clock on a Friday night, I was working late, finishing up. All that was left was to install the stereo system, and I figured that could wait until the morning. As I climbed into my truck to drive home, I took one last, longing look at the houseboat. I took the photo of Cole I keep on my speedometer and kissed it.

"Son, Daddy hopes he has pleased you. I've done my best."

I hit the ignition and the radio came on. The song that was playing was "Wind Beneath My Wings," the very song Chase had requested to be sung at Cole's funeral. I sat there and cried through the whole song.

I couldn't sleep. About one o'clock I got up and went back to the shop. I fired up the generator on the boat and by three o'clock I'd hooked up the stereo system. I took a breath and hit the button to see if it would work. "Wind Beneath My Wings" came on the radio. Again I sat down and cried through the whole song.

EIGHTEEN

God Shows Up

I LEFT OUT ONE SMALL DETAIL about the night before I moved the houseboat to the shop.

Cole paid me a visit.

Chase had gone out with some of his friends, and Judy was waiting up for him. I knew it would be a pretty tough day getting that boat to the shop, so I hit the sack early.

I'd barely fallen asleep when I heard Cole call my name.

"Where are you, Son, in Austin?"

"No, Dad, I'm right here."

"You're at Caren's apartment?"

"No, Dad, I'm right here by you."

All of a sudden, I could see him, I could smell him and I could taste him. As I kissed his head, he dropped it down on my chest and he shook.

He said, "Dad, I'm so sorry."

"It's okay," I said. "It was an accident. We'll be okay."

I woke up and looked at his picture that the University of Texas had given us. I got out of bed. I walked over and kissed that picture, and I promised him that I wouldn't do the what-ifs or the only-ifs anymore. I would just enjoy those twenty-one years of memories that he had given me.

People ask me how I handle the pain of losing my son. I tell them I don't have much of a choice. I either let the pain embitter me, or I let it better me. Embitterment is so miserable.

I don't duck the pain. I *won't* duck the pain. I think of embracing the pain like squeezing a puppy. Squeeze it too tight and it'll go away.

Sometimes I feel that the more I hurt, the more I love him. I still drive Highway 79 to Austin. Coming and going, I pass the spot where my son crashed. Every time I drive that road, every time I see the big concrete silo that marks the crash site on the horizon I feel that knot in my stomach. Every time I pass it, I pull to the side of the road, get out and walk down by the cross, sit on the guardrail and just think.

Some people think of a cemetery out in the middle of the woods as an eerie place. So did I. Now I find it a place of peace, even in the middle of the still, dark night. When I sit on the grass at Fellowship Cemetery of Dubberly and talk to my son, I don't know if he's out there somewhere listening to me. I would like to think he is. But I do know that I always feel better afterwards. If you can do something that is going to make you feel better, shouldn't you do it?

The reason that I continue to drive hours to the wreck site or go sit in the cemetery in the middle of the night is because of the Love Wars. I wish people would just buy into the Love Wars and know that it's not how much someone loves you, but how much you love them. Loving someone unconditionally is such a wonderful feeling. Because my son's gone, should I love him any less? Because he's gone, should I just forget about him?

I don't consider myself an intelligent man, but that's not the reason I don't ask why. I don't deal with the whys because I can't change them. Why dwell on something over which I have absolutely no control? That may have been one of the hardest obstacles to overcome when I heard about Cole's death. I'm a carpenter by trade, good with my hands. Until my son died, there wasn't anything I couldn't fix. I had always been able to do something about everything, but I could do absolutely nothing to ease my pain, or to ease Chase's pain or to ease Judy's pain.

The what-ifs are tempting. Cole had a promising career in football. He had a beautiful and loving fiancée in Caren. He would have been one of the greatest daddies ever. But for my own sanity I have to put up a wall that what-ifs can't bust through, because if I stop and think about the what-ifs even for a short period of time, I know they will destroy me.

In a way I'm lucky, and I know it. People knew my son. They loved my son.

We received cards and letters from people all across the country. The governor of Texas, the president of the United States. The Notre Dame and Penn State football teams. We've gotten scribbled letters from young kids who met Cole at their school and from a lady who saw him talking to a small boy at the San Diego Airport in the early morning hours after the Longhorns' loss to Oregon.

About three weeks after Cole's death, Judy was at home when a middle-aged stranger called. The man was very emotional.

"Mrs. Pittman, you don't know me, but every day I pray for your family over your loss of Cole. Every day, Mrs. Pittman, I cry. Cole Pittman was so special to me. I had met him on several occasions in the parking garage at the University of Texas. Mrs. Pittman, Cole always made me feel like I was somebody special. Cole always had time to stop and visit with me."

There was an awkward pause.

"Mrs. Pittman, I have done something that is so stupid. I went and got a tattoo of a Longhorn on my arm. In that Longhorn I put the number forty-four so I could have a part of your son with me for the rest of my life."

We are blessed.

Judy and I appreciate the kind words and letters, but there are times it gets to us. Recently I had a guy come and sit next to me and tell me he knew what I was feeling. He had lost his father that year, and he was having a tough time. I was trying to be nice, but I had to work really hard on being nice because the guy was making me mad. I buried my daddy, and it took me thirteen years to get over it. I buried my mom, my sister, a niece, nephew, cousins and all my grandparents. But as far as I was concerned, you could take all of these wonderful people who I was raised with and who I was close to and multiply it by a billion and it wouldn't scratch the surface of burying Cole Pittman. No, he didn't know how I felt. I can't even say I know how Judy feels.

Even after losing my son, I would not approach someone else who had lost his child and tell him I know what he's going through, because I don't. Everyone's loss is special. Everyone grieves differently. Everyone feels different emotions. Everyone will have to handle it differently. Now when I try to comfort someone who's bereaved, I just offer a compassionate hug or a prayer. I'll tell them I've got them on my heart, and I'm there if they need me. If they feel like they need to talk, I'm willing to listen. It's just showing you care that's important.

When I heard of Cole's death, I thought immediately of the Jabez prayer. I looked to the sky and recited it in total sarcasm.

I mocked God for having done what he did to enlarge Cole's territory.

I was truly angry for less than a minute.

Man made the fast cars. Man made vehicles as a means of transportation; they have their good side, and they have their bad side. Cole knew the dangers of falling asleep, but it was his decision not to pull over and take a nap. I don't think it's God's responsibility to run around zapping everybody out of harm's way on a regular basis.

At one time I thought of God as a supernatural being, speaking the world into existence, raining judgment on evildoers.

Now I see God as a comforter, and I'll tell you why.

Experiencing the death of a child is the most horrific pain someone on this earth can experience. You're just looking for a way to survive, the pain is so unbearable.

I was looking, and God showed up.

Whenever I was at my lowest, God showed up. When I was searching for words to eulogize my son, God showed up. It was obvious when he did. Strength entered me, physically and mentally, and I began to reflect.

I began to think of children as they go through the everyday motions of life. How we, as parents, just go through the motions. But let one of our children stumble, and we are there immediately to lift them up, to strengthen them.

God was doing the same with me as I did with my children.

He was grieving as I grieved, but I felt strength when I needed it. We can try as hard as a human being possibly can, but God always wins the Love War.

That statement leads to a confession. Since Cole's death, many people have talked to me about how I handled his death differently from other people they know who've lost children. I am going to tell you why. I am going to tell you why these people think I've embraced the pain.

Every time I struggle, God shows up. The feeling is so profound, so unique and so special. I've come to where I like having God around. Because of Cole's death I no longer think of God as that Supreme Being, but more of God as the Father.

After all, didn't God make us in his image? What pleases us is what pleases God. Nothing is more special to me then when my kids come and just hang out with me. So now on a regular basis, I just kind of hang out with God. It allows me to see us as God sees us. God said in the Bible that we were made in his image, but what does that mean? We all look different. Which one of us looks the most like God?

God, I've come to believe, was talking about our souls. Our souls are made in God's image. We do not pay much attention to our souls. Neither do we pay much attention to our fingers, our hands or our eyes until they are bruised or battered. Then that part of our physical being becomes important. When you bury your son, your soul is bruised. God is the only source of comfort to ease that pain. That is why I embrace the pain, because God shows up and helps me through it.

I still recite the Prayer of Jabez, though I don't say it every day, and I wouldn't dare pray it over Chase. Now, when I say it, I say it over myself, because I no longer have any fear of death. I have realized my worst fear. How can I possibly be afraid of anything?

NINETEEN

"All You Need to Say"

CHASE HAD LIVED IN HIS older brother's shadow, searching for his own direction. When Cole died, Chase lost his best friend. He was hurting, and he was grasping for a way to channel his grief.

Every spring, Evangel has a Lift-a-Thon where the players get people to pledge money for each pound they can bench press. The money goes to pay expenses for the football team.

Chase needed encouragement, and he needed focus. The Lift-a-Thon was the chance to provide both. Evangel had never had a player bench four-hundred pounds. I challenged him to be the first.

I had him benching a large sum of weight, but I was keeping my hands on the bar so he never knew how much he was lifting. The idea came from Jeff "Mad Dog" Madden, the strength and conditioning coach at the University of Texas, who called it over-training. When I felt sure Chase could lift four-hundred pounds, I told him so. He thought it was impossible. We were still about a month away from the Lift-a-Thon. I put 405 on the bar. As I dropped it down to his chest, I quickly stepped back. He powered it up, and we celebrated. The four-hundred-pound mark was not only in reach, it had been passed.

Chase was also training at Evangel, and on Mondays, the day that we benched, they ran this huge, man-made hill. On those days Chase was his weakest. One Monday afternoon, only a week and a half out from the Lift-a-Thon, we got to 365 pounds. He was struggling.

"Dad, this is not a good day," he said.

Lifting heavy weights is almost as much psychological as physical. I was afraid that if I put the 405 pounds on there and he missed it, he would develop a mental block that he couldn't bench it. So instead of going to 405, I went to 415. I felt like if he missed the 415, then he would still have it in his head he could do 405.

Chase popped right up with 415.

For a high school junior to be able to bench press four-hundred pounds is phenomenal. Not many college players in America can do that, nor many pro players either.

We weren't stopping there. I told Chase that it went up so easy that he had to put 425 on the bar. By then a large group of people had gathered. Basically everybody in the club had stopped to watch.

Once again he exploded the weight off his chest and benched the 425. Tuesday was bench press day at Evangel, and they lift the first period of the school day. When he arrived at Evangel the next morning, he was still riding high from the evening before. He put 405 on the bar and did it three times. He put 425 on and did it once.

Chase went straight for the phone.

"Dad," he told me, "I will bench 440 pounds to honor my brother."

Now I've got to tell you, I was excited he would try to do that for his brother, but I was also worried he had set a goal that couldn't be reached. I'd been working out in the gym for many years. I had never seen anybody but a professional power lifter with a thick chest and short arms to bench this kind of weight.

The day of the Lift-a-Thon came. They had five benches set up in the gym to accommodate the football team. Chase was at the heavy bench, where the larger players lifted. He told me he had been sick to his stomach all day from nerves, but he was up to the challenge. Personally, I was just hoping he could get the 405. I'd watched kids lift in previous years, and I knew that the combination of nerves and all that attention meant they almost never did as well in the competition as when they were just training in the weight room. There were about three hundred people in the gym, and word had gone out about Chase's 425-pound bench. He was on the spot.

After warming up, Chase opened at 405. He struggled but made it. I upped it to 415.

"Son, you've done a phenomenal thing," I told him. "The best lifter at Evangel had only done 385 pounds. You've gotten 405. If you get 415, you get it. If you don't, you don't."

The 415 went up easily.

I knew he only had a limited amount of heavy lifts in him, and I worried 425 would take too much out of him. I took the 5-pound plate off each end and put a 10-, a 5- and a 2½-pound plate next to the four 45-pound plates on each side. It was at 440 pounds.

I was spotting him. I lifted it off, I gave it to him, and I stepped back to make sure no one would think I was helping him. He lowered it to his chest and exploded with it. He came up about two thirds of the way, paused the bar and then easily pushed it the rest of the way up.

Head Coach Dennis Dunn had announced that Chase was going to try 440 pounds to honor his brother's uniform number. As Chase extended his arms, the spectators erupted in applause.

The next day I asked Chase why he paused with the bar two thirds of the way up. "When I got it to where I felt like I could just hold it forever, I wanted to roll my head back and look in your eyes as I lifted it the rest of the way," Chase said.

Chase lifted more than a steel bar and some iron plates off his chest that day. Bench pressing 440 pounds allowed him to take a big step as a young man, but I believe it also helped him turn a corner in dealing with his grief.

Chase and I were pulling closer and closer together as best friends. But I was still his daddy, he was still my son, and we still had to deal with the everyday trials of life.

Louisiana State was recruiting Chase hard, and we were planning to go to the spring game. Now I'm a stickler on being punctual, and I explained to Chase that we would need to leave at eight o'clock that morning.

Eight o'clock came, and he wasn't ready. I was furious. Chase barely had time to throw some clothes in a bag and hustle out to the car. I spent the first hundred miles reaming him out. The second fifty he spent sulking. I didn't let up. If he was going to go to college, he had to be self-reliant.

I could see by the look in his eye that it wasn't taking.

I had to get his attention.

We were rolling down the interstate near Alexandria when I spied an upcoming overpass.

"Son, I know I've been fussing at you, and I know you're not listening, but let me ask you one question: If we were to hit that bridge and you were killed, do you know I could stand over you and say the exact same things I said about Cole? That I had said all I needed to say? That I wouldn't need to call you back to tell you I loved you? All I've done is what daddies are supposed to do. It is my job to discipline you. If I don't discipline you, then I am not being a good daddy.

"Now keeping that statement in mind, if we hit that bridge and I was the one that got killed, would you want to call Daddy back to say something to him?"

I got through to him. That big old hand eased over and took my hand. He held my hand the rest of the way to LSU.

On the way back that evening he reached over and took my hand. "I was a rear end this morning, wasn't I?" he said.

I explained to him that was okay. That as long as you can find something good in something bad, as long as you can learn from the situation, it's not all bad.

TWENTY

Forty-Four for
Forty-Four

FOOTBALL WAS OUR BALM THAT fall, our saving grace. We knew it was going to be difficult for Judy and me, and we were concerned about how Chase would handle it. He had been strong, handling the sorrow with quiet grace, but we knew it might be different when it came time to honor his brother on his football field.

After Cole graduated, another player had worn number forty-four at Evangel. When Cole died, school officials decided they would honor him by retiring his jersey number, but not until Chase wore it for the first game. He wanted a Pittman to be the last one to wear the number forty-four jersey at Evangel.

When he met me for the traditional game-day lunch at Monjunis, a local Italian restaurant, he was wearing Cole's jersey. It was customary for the players to wear the game jersey to school on game day. Seeing Chase wearing that familiar jersey brought back a flood of memories. All the times I had met Cole there for lunch, he was wearing that jersey. I prayed for strength just to get through that day.

When Chase left me, instead of going back to school, he drove the forty-five miles east to Cole's grave. There he sat for an hour and a half.

During pregame ceremonies that night, a team manager found me in the stands and told me I needed to come to the locker room. It was Chase. When I got there he was crying so hard he couldn't talk. I held him and cried with him, begging God to give us the strength to make it through that night.

Chase pulled himself together. He dried his tears and tightened his chinstrap. Then he went out and played the game of his life.

The University of Texas players had already put black stickers with the initials "CP" on their helmets and kept Cole's locker just the way he left it. The school started a scholarship endowment in Cole's name and deemed that nobody would wear number forty-four until Cole would have graduated.

Mack Brown wanted to do more. He wanted to honor Cole with a special ceremony before a home game, so they selected September 8, 2001, a day the Longhorns would be playing Mack's former team, the North Carolina Tar Heels.

We were honored, but we had a bit of a logistical problem. Evangel was scheduled to play a Friday night game in Monroe, about two hours east of Shreveport. Kickoff for the North Carolina game was set for eleven o'clock Saturday morning. Mack, worried about an all-night drive, arranged for us to catch a plane in Monroe and fly to Austin. It wasn't easy, because Chase was considered a potential recruit and the NCAA has strict rules about paid visits. But Texas, through some lobbying with the NCAA, came through.

I could tell it was going to be a special weekend when we got to Monroe. There was a solitary cloud in the sky, and it was shaped like a Longhorn. Evangel dominated the game against Ouachita, building a forty-point halftime lead. Our starters never saw the field in the second half. Flush with victory and a little on edge over what awaited us at Royal-Memorial Stadium, we boarded the plane to Austin.

Mack had made arrangements to have us picked up at the airport and carried to the Capitol Marriott, the team hotel, where the next morning we had breakfast with the team. We began to try to prepare ourselves for a day of mixed emotions, but that was impossible. When we walked out of the tunnel and onto the field, eighty-three thousand fans were cheering and waving. Before the game Mack gathered the team around Judy, Chase and me and presented us with a framed jersey and a scrapbook that the Texas Angels support group traditionally prepared from the day that a scholarship football player arrived on campus until the day he graduates. They had a special surprise: Cole's "T" ring. A "T" ring is a treasure coveted by Longhorn athletes and given only to those who earn their degree. They had made an exception in Cole's case.

On the JumboTron they showed a video of the speech he made when he committed to Texas, right down to the end where he said it wasn't just about football but about promoting Jesus Christ.

I later heard from a couple in Tennessee, watching the presentation on television, who accepted Jesus after listening to that video.

Texas kicked off and held the Tar Heels on downs, but then had to punt. When North Carolina got the ball back, their quarterback tried to hit a quick slant. Texas defensive coordinator Carl Reese called a stunt that had end Cory Redding dropping in coverage.

Cory was one of Cole's best friends. One night in Dead Man's Talk Cole had talked to me about some of the personal problems that Cory was dealing with. I don't think Cory will ever know just how much Cole loved him. Cole cried on the phone that night because of what Cory was going through. Since then, I've kept a close eye on Cory. I don't think Cory knows that I see some of the things that he still does to commemorate my son, from kissing the CP sticker on his helmet to putting his finger on the CP and pointing to the sky after a big game. Cory has touched my heart forever.

The North Carolina quarterback, confused by the stunt, threw the ball right to where Cory was standing. Cory intercepted it and raced down the sideline as the quarterback, who had the angle on him, came over to cut him off. Not knowing how athletic Cory was, the quarterback went for his legs. Cory expected that from a quarterback. He simply somersaulted over him, leaving the ground at the four-yard-line and landing flat on his back in the end zone.

It was almost surreal how many of Cole's closest friends played a big part in the game. With Texas leading 38–14 late in the fourth quarter, linebacker Reed Boyd, a good old country boy like Cole who came to Texas in the same recruiting class, intercepted a Tar Heel pass.

Texas drove down the field. With thirty-six seconds left, another buddy of Cole's, Brett Robin, dove over for a touchdown. I was excited as anyone with the prospect of a big win on such a special day. I was so caught up in the festivities and emotion that I had no idea what had just happened. I didn't even look at the scoreboard.

Thank God Chance Mock did. Chance was Cole's best friend. After Cole died, Chance wore the old hunting jacket that Cole used to wear. It was too big for a little ol' quarterback, but he wore it anyway. I wanted it back but I didn't have the heart to ask him for it, because Chance meant so much to us too. Cole called us at nine-thirty every night. When Cole died, it was Chance who called at nine-thirty every night.

Aside from being Cole's suitemate, Chance was also the Longhorns' third-team quarterback, which meant he was the guy standing next to the coaches charting plays. After the touchdown he made a beeline for Mack Brown. As the extra point team trotted on the field he pointed at the scoreboard. Mack understood.

Under Texas it read "44."

Major Applewhite stepped under center, got the snap and took a knee. All around us, fans turned to us and held up both hands, each with four fingers extended.

It would end at 44-14.

After the final gun we headed down to the field. Weeping, we hugged every player and every coach we could. The players surrounded Judy and Chase and me as we walked back across the field to the locker room. It took Mack a few minutes to get the players settled down so he could give his postgame speech, but then he presented us with the game ball.

I told the players that "Beating North Carolina was one NC for Cole Pittman. Let's get one more NC before the season ends." I didn't have to mention that NC stood for national championship.

Judy was so emotional she could hardly talk. She just told the players how much she loved them.

Chase pointed at the football team. "I'll see you in January," was all he said. He was going to follow his big brother to Texas.

We hugged everyone in sight, and then it was time to head back to the hotel. Mack had arranged a car for us, but the Texas fans had been so great we just wanted to walk back through their midst, thanking as many of them as we could.

They surrounded us. We hugged some more. We autographed programs they presented to us. I wanted to stop at the tailgate party sponsored by *Hornfans.com*, a fan-based UT website that had been so supportive of us. The owners, Katy and Robert Agnor, had been instrumental in helping us raise funds for the Cole Pittman Memorial Fieldhouse at Evangel, and we wanted to go by and hug them and let them join in our celebration. Robert was behind the grill, cooking for the fans. Tears ran down his face as he hugged me and kissed me. We would have stayed forever, but we had a dinner date and time was running short.

We still had a good half-mile to walk, so I decided we needed to catch a cab. I stepped out to the street and there was a yellow minivan taxi. As we climbed into the back seat, exhausted, the cab driver started a conversation.

"Man, how about forty-four points for number forty-four,

Cole Pittman?" he said excitedly. "What an awesome kid this must have been."

I knew this guy hadn't been to the football game, so he must have been listening on the radio.

"Wasn't it awesome?" I said.

He looked back over his shoulder and sized me up.

"You look like you may have played football. Are you a parent to one of the players? Have you ever met this guy, Cole Pittman?"

I nodded. "We are his parents," I said quietly.

The man started weeping. He wept all the way back to the hotel. The last thing he said was, "I only wish I could say for sure, I had given an individual like Cole Pittman a ride one time."

I tried to give him his fare. He wouldn't take it. I had to leave it there on the backseat.

That taxicab driver will never know how much he blessed us that day.

We were all wiped out, physically and in spirit, but I looked forward to the morning. We had been invited to the Morning Star Christian Church, where Cole frequently attended. There, in front of the whole congregation, I had an opportunity to explain to people why I couldn't be mad at God.

On the flight home we looked at the scrapbook, and we admired the treasures that Texas had presented us. There is no way in my life that I'll ever be able to share the feelings in my heart toward Mack Brown and the University of Texas. That

football team, Governor of Texas Rick Perry, the whole state of
Texas—there's no way I'd ever be able to express how much
they have helped us survive.

—⚬∿⚬—

When I talked to the team in the locker room after the North
Carolina game, I talked about getting two NCs. It was now
October 6. Texas was playing defending national champion
Oklahoma at the Cotton Bowl in Dallas, and there was one task
at hand.

You've got to beat the king to be the king.

By now I felt I had reason to believe that Texas was destined
for that second NC, a national championship. Governor Perry
had invited me to sit with him in his suite at the Cotton Bowl. I
accepted. I had Chase and his girlfriend Britni with me, and we
were to meet George Hawthorne, a good friend of mine, before
the game. I was feeling about as good as someone could feel
after losing a child. There was no way Texas was going to lose
this ballgame. I had no doubt we were a much better team than
Oklahoma.

Again we were blessed. Fans went out of their way to show
me how much they loved my son. A small boy came up to me,
just wanting to hug me and shake my hand. People from everywhere were hugging me and shaking my hand as I made my

way to where the buses dropped the players off at the locker room. We were running late, and a couple thousand fans were already lined up waiting. They weren't budging. Two security police in a golf cart had to force their way through the crowd, all but pushing people out of the way with the cart. There was nowhere to move. When the crowd had closed back up and the police had passed through, a fan turned around and noticed me standing there.

"There's Mr. Pittman," he said. The most unbelievable thing happened. The crowd opened up, not just wide enough for me to pass through, but wide enough to drive an eighteen-wheeler through. I made my way to the front so I could wave and even touch some of the players' hands as they made their way to the dressing room.

Chase was on his official recruiting visit, so he, Britni and George went around to be with the recruits. I took my place beside the governor. We had a great visit. It was a great game. Only one thing was wrong. Texas didn't win.

On the drive back to Shreveport I knew I had to write Mack Brown a letter.

This is what I wrote:

Dear Coach:

At the beginning of the season after losing Cole, I allowed myself to fantasize about winning the National

Championship with CP on the helmet. It would have allowed Cole to be a part of Texas' rich history and tradition. It would have also helped me keep his memory alive.

With Texas dominating the first games and with a 44–14 score at the North Carolina game it became more than a fantasy. It seemed as though Cole had put his stamp on it and it was going to happen. After Oklahoma defeated us, my heart was so heavy I didn't think my feet would carry me back around to where the players were boarding the bus. No one could have wanted to win this game more than I did. At least that was my thoughts, until the players came out. As I hugged some of the players with their heads down, I could feel their pain and then going into the locker room and seeing you, Coach. You and that team were feeling the same way I was.

I was already dreading the drive home. I knew I would be doing what I always do in the dark of the night where no one can see me. I cry. I knew it would be a painful journey to the house. I was only partly right. As darkness settled in, tears begin to roll down my face and I began to think about Cole. I begin to question why. After all, I lost my son. Would it be too much to win the National Championship with CP on the helmet?

*Would there be no end to the pain I feel? I was travel-
ing the road of despair, feeling sorry for myself and the
University of Texas.*

*Then a strange thing happened. I think Cole was at
that football game, and I think God was allowing him to
speak to me because my thoughts went as this: "Dad, do
you remember the first thing Coach Brown said to me
when we visited the University of Texas?" He said,
"Son, we are offering you a scholarship, not because
you are a great football player, but because you are a
great football player with character. If you were the best
football player in America and you didn't have character, you would have no place at the University of Texas."*

*Then I felt in my spirit as he told me, "Dad, haven't
you always told me that life wasn't fair? If life was fair,
I would have been at the game with you tonight, playing for the University of Texas. Dad, haven't you
always taught me that the best team doesn't always
win? Tonight, the best team didn't win. Haven't you
always taught me that if you can find something good
in something bad, then it's not all bad? Well, tonight,
the good far outweighed the bad, because tonight was
about character.*

*"Success is not a character builder, adversity is. Did
you see my teammates tonight, did you see my coaches*

*tonight? I'm so proud of them. If we had won tonight's
game or even if we had won the National Championship, it would have lasted a year. Next year people
would want the same.*

*"You will never be able to measure the effects of
tonight's game, but I can see the big picture. What those
boys went through tonight will prepare them for a lifetime, and from generation to generation, character that
was built because of this loss will eventually be a Texas
victory.*

*"Which would you rather have, National Champions
for a year or World Champions for a lifetime?"*

*Cole taught me many things in his lifetime and I'm
so grateful that he can still teach me things in his death.
The tears stopped and I began to see things in a different light about adversity. I can now understand why
walk-ons, though never having playing time on the
field, will benefit themselves and the University of
Texas because of the adversity they face. I began to see
the good in things such as injuries and players realiz-
ing they are just one play away from not playing. You
need to prepare yourself for other things in life.*

*We would all do well to remember what Cole said
when he committed to Texas. "It's not just about
football."*

TWENTY-ONE

I Love You So Much

DURING FOOTBALL SEASON MY WEEKEND calendar was full. We'd go watch Chase play on Friday night, get an early start Saturday and drive to wherever Texas was playing to watch Cole.

After Cole died I'd still go to the Longhorn home games, but on the weekends when they were on the road, there was time to fill.

I spent much of it at the hunting lease with my buddies. It didn't matter what game was in season. I wasn't hunting anything but peace and understanding.

One weekend in October 2001, I arrived at the hunting lease and found that some new deer stands had been put up in the area where I normally hunt. Instead, I went to one of my friends' spots toward the back of the lease.

No one took a shot at any game all afternoon, and as darkness settled in I crawled on my four-wheeler to make my way back to the camp. As I drove I began to think about Cole. I began to think about how much he enjoyed that hunting lease. I began to think about the times we had together. I began to think about Dead Man's Talk and where it originated. I had decided to tackle my sadness head-on, to embrace it as best as I could, but grief has a manner of hitting you in ways you can't anticipate, can't control.

In the weeks after Cole had died, there was no end to the cards, letters and calls from people trying to help us through our grief. As time passed, the cards, letters and calls dwindled. The pain did not. Sitting in the deer blind, I realized how I hadn't understood when one of my brothers lost his daughter, or when another brother lost his stepson. I didn't realize the pain they felt, the kind that causes you to pull over to the side of the road so you can throw up, the kind that caused me to lay down next to my son's headstone and talk to him for hours on end.

As I rode the four-wheeler back to the cabin, the chill set in the night air, and the chill set in on my bones. By the time I had arrived at the camp, I was crying.

As I pulled the four-wheeler up on its trailer, my hunting buddies gathered around me. It was dark, and I had my head down.

They wanted to know if I'd seen anything. Did I shoot anything? I was so emotional I couldn't answer them for a few moments. They began to realize I was crying.

I tried to tell them what I was feeling. I tried to thank them for the wonderful memories. I tried to remind them to cherish the moments they had. I tried to tell them how special they were to me.

I had always been the tough guy at the lease—the hunter, the outdoorsman, the rugged one, the one that came from a hard background. I don't think they had ever seen me cry, not even at Cole's funeral.

When I left the hunting lease that night, I didn't go home. I made my way to the cemetery and knelt by Cole's grave. The pain was almost unbearable, the emptiness overwhelming. I cried out to God, I begged God to ease my pain. I cried out to Cole, screaming aloud how much I loved him. I thought maybe if I screamed loud enough he would hear me through the curtain of death that had separated us.

I'm not sure how long I stayed there that night, and I don't remember everything I said. But as I turned to walk off, I stopped. I walked back to his grave.

"Son, Daddy would give anything in the world if he could just one more time hear you tell him, 'Dad, I love you so much.'"

Cole had already heard me.

Months earlier, about three weeks after Cole's death, I was leaving the gym one morning when my cell phone rang. It was Bob Lyons, Caren's father, calling from Houston.

His voice was tentative. Something was up.

"Marc, I need to tell you something," he started.

I cut in. "I need to tell you something too," I said. And I begin to thank him for sharing his family with mine, for allowing Caren to be a part of our lives and for allowing Caren to stay with us some after Cole's death.

He interrupted me.

"Marc, I've got to tell you something," he said.

"What is it?" I said.

"Caren is pregnant."

Now I'm from the old Christian school and wasn't sure how I was supposed to feel. I thought of what people might think about Cole fathering a child out of wedlock. I worried about him not being here to defend himself to critics. Would it hurt the baby? Would it hurt Caren? Would it dishonor my son? Deep down, I've got to tell you, my heart was beating a hundred miles an hour. There were a million thoughts racing through my mind.

"Bob, how does Caren feel about that?"

"Marc, she is excited."

"Bob, how do you and Sue feel about that?"

"Marc, we think it's a miracle. We would love nothing more

than to know we were going to have a grandson or grandchild that has the qualities that Cole Pittman had."

I then asked him if he would hold on so I could turn some cartwheels. But as excited as I was, when I gave Judy the news she was just beside herself with happiness. Knowing Caren was having Cole's baby was what kept Judy going over the next few months.

Our first concern, of course, was Caren. She had struggled emotionally so much with Cole's death, we were afraid she would have a miscarriage. To be honest, we didn't know how it could be possible that she could still be carrying this baby. The first trimester was difficult. She had morning sickness every day, but that probably wasn't the worst of it. Judy and I were hovering over her and wearing the phone out when we were not around her. This baby had become the most important thing in the world to us.

As the baby grew and Caren passed through the first trimester it became evident that we would need to start telling people that Caren was pregnant with Cole's baby. I began mentally rehearsing things I would say and how I would say them. I was even justifying in my own mind an unwed pregnancy.

The reasoning was simple. In my heart I felt that God had blessed us with this child because Cole had lived a good life, been kind to children and was always a willing witness for Jesus Christ. Because of the way we had handled Cole's death and had not become angry or bitter with God, he had blessed us with this child. I thought of the Prayer of Jabez and how this might be how Cole's territory would be enlarged.

Still, I was worried about what people would think of Caren or what people would think of Cole. The last thing I wanted to do was tarnish his name or Caren's character, so we kept it very quiet, not telling anyone outside of the immediate family.

An amazing thing happened. As we prepared to expand the circle to include a very close friend of mine, who also happens to be a preacher, he interrupted me.

"Caren is pregnant," he said.

I was stunned. "How do you know?"

He reached out to me. "We've been praying for it diligently," he said.

As the word began to spread, many other people told us that they had been praying for it. That made us feel better, but we still had to tell our pastor, Denny Duron. I worried over how he would handle it, what he would say.

Denny was sitting with another Evangel assistant coach, Johnny Booty, when I broke the news to both of them. They wept, assuring me it was a gift from God. I needed to hear this. It did my soul good. I needed to know that Caren wouldn't be judged and my son wouldn't be judged.

Truth was, I wasn't beyond some unfair judgment of my own. I wanted a grandson, pure and simple, and I was certain I would get one, just as I was certain I would have two boys. So when we went with Caren for the ultrasound that would reveal the baby's sex, I looked at it as a mere formality.

They looked and looked, but they didn't find the equipment that I was sure they would find.

Disappointment was all over my face. I couldn't hide it. Caren couldn't hide her disappointment, either, but it had nothing to do with the baby's sex. She was upset, even angry with me that I was so obviously disappointed that it wasn't a boy. By the look on my face it was clear that a girl just wouldn't do. A girl couldn't grow up to be all I wanted my grandson to be. A girl couldn't carry on the Pittman name. I had just lost my son. I wanted him back. I wanted another Cole Pittman. Who wouldn't?

Ever since Cole's death Judy and I had looked for signs from Cole that everything would be all right. The sign we asked for was for his jersey number, forty-four, to appear. Cole had worn that number when he was a running back his first year of organized football, carried it with him to Evangel, where he wore forty-four in football, baseball and basketball, and on to the University of Texas.

Judy asked Cole to send us some forty-fours.

We must have received forty-four hundred forty-fours. As we drove off we saw it as the first digits on the addresses of the buildings we passed. We saw it on license plates and in phone numbers on billboards. I swear that within a mile we saw a hundred forty-fours.

I got the message. A complete peace came over me, but that wasn't all I felt. I was struck with the realization of how foolish I'd been, how selfish I'd been. I knew that it couldn't be a boy, it had to be a girl. No boy could live up to what I wanted a grandson to be. He would not only have to be like Cole, he'd have to be even better than Cole. If Cole were strong, he'd have to be stronger. As fast as Cole was, he'd have to be faster. As tough and personable and honest and loving as Cole was, my grandson would have to be tougher and more personable and more honest, with an even greater capacity to love and be loved.

There will never be another Cole Pittman.

My son isn't done teaching me yet.

*I*t is the wee hours of October 16, 2001. The phone rings. It's Sue, Caren's mother.

"Y'all need to come on," she says urgently. "Caren is having labor contractions."

We live three-and-a-half hours from Houston. We drive in separate vehicles because Judy knows that when that baby is born, she will not want to come back. I have Chase with me and he will have to be back for practice and a ball game that week.

By the time we arrive in Houston and make our way to the hospital, Caren's labor contractions have stopped. They've given her something to ease her pain, and it seems to have slowed and then stopped her labor. Chase and I hang around for the remainder of the day. An exam shows that Caren is fine, that this was just false labor. Judy, though, decides the baby is coming soon and she's going to stay. Chase and I hug them all good-bye and head back to Shreveport.

Two days pass. It's now October 18, early morning on a Thursday. Evangel is getting ready for a rare Thursday night game when the phone rings. It's Judy. They're at the hospital. It looks like today's the day.

I hang the phone up and lay there in the dark, weighing my options. I can drive to Houston and leave Chase there, but I might not have time to be back to support him at the ballgame tonight. There is no guarantee the baby will be born today. It could just be another false alarm. And even if the baby is born, what difference would it make if I am there? Chase and I can both go tomorrow and stay the weekend. I've all but convinced myself to stay.

Then I turn to look at the clock.

It is 4:44 A.M.

I shoot upright. "Son, just hold on," I shout out loud. "I'm on my way."

I jump in the shower, get dressed, kiss Chase bye and tell him I will be back in time for his game. I head for Houston. As I drive, I think about what I will say. What could I say that would represent Cole? What could I say that would be as profound to me as the first words I spoke when he was born? "My Son, My Son, My Son." Those are words that are chiseled near the base of his gravestone, words that are etched on his cross at his memorial site.

I can think of nothing. The only thing that keeps me going is the feeling that when I hold that baby, I'll know what to say.

I drive as fast as I can and I arrive at the hospital about four minutes before Payton Cole Pittman. When they call us into the room and Judy hands me that precious baby girl, I understand why I couldn't think of anything to say.

After they take the baby back, I am overcome with an urgency to leave. There is somewhere I have to go, and it isn't Shreveport. It is Fellowship Cemetery of Dubberly, where my son's body lies.

Stopping only to gas up, I make my way to the cemetery. Every time I had approached his grave when I was alone, I would weep. This time as I approach his grave, I am smiling.

Death ends a life, not a relationship. Death begins only when we're forgotten. That's why I speak to so many church groups and Texas Exes gatherings and anybody else who'll hear my message. That's why I drive three hours each way to a lonely stretch of Highway 79 just to wipe down a burnt orange cross. That's why last January 26, the day my boy would have turned twenty-two, I went to Fellowship Cemetery with some news articles and a box of his favorite Cotton's Fried Chicken and sat near his grave, just talking to my best friend. That's why I wrote this book.

I don't want my son to die.

For most of the last twenty-two years I've done everything I can to win the Love Wars, and I don't feel I'm done fighting yet. But I know in this, Cole can't be beaten. He gave me—he gave us—little Payton Cole Pittman.

Even I finally got it through my thick skull. I spent so much time thinking of what to say when I held my granddaughter that I missed the real message. It wasn't my time to say anything, it was Cole's. When I held Payton Cole that day, I learned a new kind of Dead Man's Talk.

I heard Cole Pittman loud and clear one more time.

I heard him say, "Dad, I love you so much."

ACKNOWLEDGMENTS

THIS ISN'T A HOW-TO BOOK. It is a love story about the growth of the relationship between a man and his two sons. It's not just a way to tell my story, to work my way through my grief. My belief is that it takes all of us working together to raise our children. The practices of Dead Man's Talk and Love Wars and some of the other stories, both good and bad, will hopefully help you enhance your relationship with your children.

If you had asked me a few years back how I viewed my life, I would have asked you to imagine my dad's old canvas hunting coat hanging in the back porch closet of the old house where I was raised. It hung there gathering dust, tough but not very warm. It wasn't attractive and wasn't needed much. I now see things differently. Some of the world's most prized art works are splashed on canvas. An artist with a taste for beauty can turn that drab piece of canvas into something special.

God, who spoke the world into existence with a keen eye for detail and design and purpose, is the greatest artist of all. As I relived my life writing this book, I could see where God was often there, in good times and bad, through every joy and through all the pain. I don't think I ever appreciated God's presence until I buried my son. So to God, I say thank-you for being with me now. I look forward to the time we will spend together here on earth and in eternity.

To Judy, a great mother who was never jealous of my relationship with my two sons, only encouraging, I am forever grateful.

To all the people before and after my oldest son's death who have asked me to tell the story or to write the book, I say thank-you.

I want to say thank-you to Mack Brown. I could not have made it through the first year after my son's death without Mack. The heaviness in my soul was a load I could not carry alone. Mack and Sally Brown helped lighten that load by sharing the pain. Mack Brown is the most influential person in my life. What an honor to know that he has been and will be a part of both of my son's lives.

In the University of Texas football team, Cole and Chase have hundreds of brothers. How this team has honored him and reached out to this family shows character second to none. You will be a part of my life forever. And a special thanks to you, Chance Mock, for continuing the 9:30 P.M. calls that Cole made daily while he was at Texas.

Death begins when we are forgotten, and all the fans of Texas and Evangel Christian Academy and the good people of Texas and Shreveport, Louisiana, have found ways to make certain Cole will not be forgotten. Thank you for the letters of encouragement, the hugs and the sharing of yourself with us. You have been a bigger blessing than we could ever tell you.

A special thanks goes to Robert and Katy Agnor at *Hornfans.com*, who have shared my pain and also my passion to tell the story.

Wanda Allen, my business partner, has stood by me and encouraged me to tell the story even though she knew it would take my time away from work. I'm grateful to her for covering for me—and correcting my grammar and spelling so I don't look like a complete idiot.

My buddies at the hunting lease helped me customize the concept of Dead Man's Talk to raising my boys. To Mike Woodard, Pat Woodard, Marvin Jones, Barry Teague, Gary Harrison, Steve Lee, Tim Delaney and Don Rinehart—thanks for giving me no shortage of shoulders to lean on when I needed them most.

Thanks to my agent Jim Hornfischer, president of Hornfischer Literary Management, L.P., and Bret Witter, editorial director of Health Communications Inc., for believing that my story can make a positive difference in other people's lives.

To Annette Rodgers Pittman, who knows my heart and my story, I can't thank you enough for believing in me enough that you wouldn't allow me to give up on getting my message out.

Last, but certainly not least, I want to thank Mark Wangrin. I do not think our paths crossed by chance. Thanks for the encouragement. I love you, my friend.

I HOPE READING MY STORY HAS opened your eyes to improving your relationships with God, family and friends and made a positive difference in your life. You too can make a positive difference by sharing this book with other people or contributing to the following funds. These funds will allow kids who are not as fortunate as Cole to have the same opportunities to reach out and touch other people and change lives.

COLE PITTMAN MEMORIAL FUND
c/o Robert Lyons
22023-1 Mossy Oaks
Spring, TX 77389

(Funds will be used to erect a field house at Evangel Christian Academy
as a memorial to Cole. Any additional funds will be used as a
scholarship fund for underprivileged children so they will have
the same opportunities Cole was given)

or

COLE PITTMAN SCHOLARSHIP FUND
c/o The Longhorn Foundation
P.O. Box 7389
Austin, TX 78713

(Payable to: The University of Texas)

www.raisingcole.com